Hodder Gibson

Scottish Examinatio

14-

ENGLISH

Language Skills

for the
Middle Secondary Years

Mary M Firth
Andrew G Ralston

Illustrations by
Miranda Ralston

Hodder Gibson

A MEMBER OF THE HODDER HEADLINE GROUP

Orders: please contact Bookpoint Ltd, 130 Milton Park, Abingdon, Oxon OX14 4SB. Telephone: (44) 01235 827720. Fax: (44) 01235 400454. Lines are open from 9.00–6.00, Monday to Saturday, with a 24 hour message answering service. You can also order through our website www.hoddereducation.co.uk

British Library Cataloguing in Publication Data
A catalogue record for this title is available from the British Library

ISBN-10: 0–216–96017–6
ISBN-13: 978–0–716–96017–1

First Published 2001
Previously published as 14–16 English Language Skills
Impression number   10 9 8 7 6 5 4 3
Year   2008 2007 2006 2005

ISBN-10: 0–340–81417–9
ISBN-13: 978–0–340–81417–8

Impression number   10 9 8 7 6 5
Year   2008 2007 2006 2005

Published by Hodder Gibson, 2a Christie Street, Paisley PA1 1NB
Tel: 0141 848 1609; Fax: 0141 889 6315; email: hoddergibson@hodder.co.uk

Copyright © 2001 Firth & Ralston

Printed in Great Britain for Hodder Gibson, 2a Christie Street, Paisley, PA1 1NB, Scotland, UK by Martins the Printers, Berwick upon Tweed.

INTRODUCTION

This book can in some respects be viewed as a sequel to *Knowledge about Language* (published in 1996) which provides straightforward explanations of the basics of grammar, punctuation and spelling, backed up with exercises suitable for classroom use. The focus in *Knowledge About Language* reflects the emphasis on the fundamentals of standard English to be found in the National Curriculum in use in English schools and in the Scottish 5–14 programme, and is designed for use at Key Stages 2 and 3 (Secondary One and Two).

The **Writing Skills** section of the present book builds on this material and provides further practice in punctuation, sentence structure and vocabulary suitable for use at Key Stage 4 and Secondary Three and Four in Scotland. The writing of factual, narrative or personal essays is a constant feature of English work irrespective of the syllabus being followed and some general guidance on how to approach this kind of exercise is offered, together with ideas to stimulate writing and some extracts from writing by pupils in the 14–15 age range.

The **Reading Skills** section concentrates on what has traditionally been described as comprehension or interpretation work. This remains a major component of GCSE and Standard Grade examinations, although the types of questions vary from one examination board to another. Some provide passages with shorter, more specific questions while others expect pupils to write an essay in which they consider a variety of aspects of the author's style. In addition, pupils are frequently presented with two passages linked by a common theme and asked to compare the similarities and differences in the authors' treatment of that theme.

The Passages for Practice (Prose) section contains material which will help pupils acquire the skills to answer questions of all of the above types, although the exercises are not modelled exclusively on any one particular examination board's format. Even when pupils are working towards answers of the comparative essay type — such as those to be found in various GCSE papers — passages with shorter directed questions will be useful for helping pupils to identify features of style and structure. The Passages for Practice (Poetry) provide material that will be particularly useful as an introduction to 'A' Level Practical Criticism and to the Textual Analysis type of question now required in the new Scottish Higher Still syllabus at both Intermediate and Higher level.

MMF/AGR

CONTENTS

PART ONE

READING SKILLS

ADVICE ON CLOSE READING

'Close Reading' is the name now usually given to tests in which you have to show your understanding and appreciation of language. (In the past, similar exercises might be called *Interpretation* or *Comprehension* tests.)

A key word here is 'show'. It sometimes happens that you understand the text, but you still may not get very good marks. It is important that you approach the questions in the correct way so that your knowledge and understanding is given full credit.

There are **three** important rules which you must keep in mind. Failure to follow these is the commonest reason why you may fail to score well although you understand the text.

Rule 1 : Read the question carefully

You will only get full marks if you have answered exactly what the question asks for. If you misread the question, and give information which is not asked for, you will get no marks, even if what you say is true. For example, you may be directed to a particular paragraph to find an answer. If you take your answer from a *different* part of the text you are likely to get *no* marks. You will not have *shown* that you understand the particular point that the marker was looking for. It is particularly important to notice if a question has several parts. These must all be included in your answer.

Rule 2 : Use your own words

If you just copy down some words from the passage, it is likely you will get no marks, *even if it is the correct answer!* The reason for this rule is that you could pick on the right answer by chance without actually understanding what the writer means. By expressing it in your own words, you *show* your understanding. In answering a question, you should express the writer's ideas in your own words, using language that is as simple as possible. Sometimes a question makes it quite clear that *only* a quotation is required. However, such questions are not common. You may, of course, *include* some quotation to illustrate your answer. This will be necessary for questions on things like word choice or language techniques.

Rule 3 : Fit your answer to the number of marks offered

Marks can often be lost by not including enough detail in an answer worth several marks. If a question is worth only one mark you can write a fairly brief answer. However, if a question is worth more you must extend your answer in proportion. A question for four marks, for example, may look for four separate points, or two points with detailed explanations.

Getting started:

Step one: Look at the introduction which comes before the text. Very often there will be useful information, such as a brief summary of what the passage is about.

Step two: Read the passage. Your first reading may be quite a quick one to get an impression. You can then re-read carefully the sections of text the questions direct you to.

Step three: Quickly read through **all** the questions. You might mark with a tick those which you think you know the answer to after your first reading. This will give you an idea of how easy or difficult you will find the questions and also help you to see which questions are likely to take up most time.

Step four: Go back to the beginning of the questions and answer them. Apart from the more general questions which may be asked at the end, the information will be in the order in which it appears in the text. Remember to look carefully at the section of the text to which you are directed each time. Check how much time you have left every ten minutes or so. You can then try to speed up if necessary.

Step five: If you have time, read over your answers. Make an attempt at any questions you may have missed out because you didn't know the answer. You will get no marks for an empty space, but you may get some credit for a sensible guess!

Questions

Here are some of the questions pupils commonly ask during Close Reading tests.

> *When I came to question 4 I found I had already answered it in question 3. Do I have to write it out again?*

If you follow Step Three (on page 8) this should not happen, as you will know what the next question is looking for. However, you should write it again under the heading of question 4. If you are *really* short of time you might try using brackets and an arrow to show the marker you wish to transfer part of your answer.

> *Help! I don't know the answer to question 6!*

Leave a space for your answer, and go straight on to question 7. At the end come back and think again. You may have found out the answer by now. If not, have a guess — you may be lucky and guess right.

> *I have the same answer for both questions 8 and 9. Can they both be right?*

Very unlikely. Read both questions again carefully. There will be a difference in what they are asking.

Question 3 says 'Look at lines 8–10'. Part of my answer comes from line 12. Will I get any credit for it?

No.

__Must__ I answer in sentences? I'm a slow writer.

It is best to write in sentences, though you should make the sentences as brief and simple as possible. There is no need to repeat the words of the question. For example, if the question asks, 'Give a reason why Mr Smith did not like his house', you do not need to start 'One reason why Mr Smith did not like his house was because . . .' You may simply give the reason itself: 'It was on a busy road.'

Oops! I have written ten lines for my answer and I've just noticed the question is only worth one mark.

Don't worry. As long as your answer includes the information that is wanted, you will get the mark and the unnecessary details will be ignored. However, you will have wasted time and will need to speed up. Try not to make this mistake with another single mark question.

Can I use a dictionary?

This depends on the kind of test you are doing. In an informal class-work test or a homework exercise, it is a good idea to use a dictionary to help you get the answers right and also to extend your vocabulary. However, in certain exams dictionaries are not permitted. Always check with your class teacher.

Technical Terms

As well as asking questions about the meaning of what you have read, Close Reading exercises also ask about the writer's style of expression: not just *what* the passage says but *how* it says it.

Some examining boards ask you to write an essay comparing two passages of fiction or journalism. Here is a typical example:

> *"Explore the main issues in the two articles and compare the way language is being used to present them."*

To help you answer this kind of question, it is useful to know some of these technical terms.

Theme: a central idea running through the whole text, such as the theme of excessive ambition leading to a downfall in Shakespeare's 'Macbeth'.

Context: this term refers to the sentences surrounding an individual word or phrase. You may be asked to show how the context of a word affects the meaning.

Tone: the *manner* in which something is said, rather than *what* is said.

I could tell by the tone of my mother's voice that she was not going to be very pleased.

First person / third person: a story can be told from various points of view. For example, in a first person narrative (using 'I', 'me', etc.), the story is told as if the author is one of the characters:

> *It was a cold, dismal February morning when I set off on what was to be the most important journey of my life.*

Using a first person narrative allows the reader to see everything from the character's own standpoint and this is likely to make us more sympathetic to him or her.

In a third person narrative (using 'he', 'she', etc.), the story is told by an author who can see into the minds of his characters.

> *Laura had never expected to see Martin again. She was very surprised when he phoned to tell her that he had decided not to move to London after all.*

Irony: when the author or speaker means the opposite of what is actually stated. We often do this in conversation, as when someone says: 'He's a real bundle of laughs, isn't he?' when in reality the person has no sense of humour at all.

The term irony is also used to describe a situation involving unfortunate timing:

> *Ironically, Sarah had just finished writing her letter of resignation when the boss called her in and offered her a pay rise.*

Emotive language: language which reveals the writer's feelings, or which appeals to the reader's feelings. For example,

> *He is one of the most dishonest, despicable, loathsome people I have ever met!*

would be an example of emotive language, making the speaker's feelings very clear.

This example of emotive language from a charity leaflet makes an appeal to the reader's feelings:

> *Will you please give what you can to relieve the distressing plight of thousands of helpless animals who have suffered so badly at the hands of cruel and thoughtless owners?*

Jargon: technical terms used in connection with a specialised field of study. For example:

> *The insurance policy was so full of legal jargon that I could hardly understand what it meant.*

Medicine, computing and any other specialised subject area will have jargon words which are familiar to those who work in the field. The following is an example of the jargon used in the world of finance:

> *The retirement benefit obligation is measured using the projected unit credit method, which recognises future projected compensation and pension increases as well as the pensions and vested rights known at the closing date.*

(You don't need to explain what this means!)

Hyperbole: deliberate exaggeration in order to emphasise a point. For example:

> *Look at the mess your room is in! It looks like a bomb's been dropped on it!*

Formal language:

- ♦ correct grammar and sentence structures
- ♦ no shortened forms (such as don't or wouldn't)
- ♦ tends to be factual
- ♦ is more likely to be written rather than spoken

This passage is an example of formal language:

Research recently carried out at an American University suggests that children's television programmes contain approximately twenty violent acts per hour. Such findings have led many people to conclude that the behaviour of young people is greatly influenced by what they see on television and that, inevitably, violence on the screen creates further violence in real life.

Informal language:

- ♦ uses looser sentence structures
- ♦ uses abbreviations
- ♦ tends to be more personal in tone
- ♦ is more likely to be spoken English

This passage is an example of informal language:

I know everybody keeps saying 'you're a shopaholic' — and I admit it: so I am. Like when we went to America last summer. I can't remember a thing about the sightseeing tour but I can tell you all about the cool shopping malls!

Other names for this kind of style are **conversational** or **colloquial** language.

Simile: a comparison between two different things that are like each other in one or more respects. Usually, the word 'like' or 'as' is used. For example:

He dried himself with a towel that felt like sandpaper.

Metaphor: a similar kind of comparison, although in this case one thing is said to be the other, and not merely like it. For example:

A curtain of cloud hid the distant mountains from view.

Personification: a specialised kind of metaphor in which a thing is said to have the qualities of a person. Here, for example, the novelist William McIlvanney compares an evening to a corpse:

The remains of a long day lay decomposing outside.

Oxymoron: two words of opposite meaning placed side by side — as in 'controlled panic'.

Alliteration: the use of two or more words beginning with the same letter (as in 'curtain of cloud').

TITANIC (1): THE MOVIE

In the course of its maiden voyage to New York in 1912, the White Star Liner 'Titanic' struck an iceberg. Of the 2,207 people on board, only 705 survived.

As the luggage was being loaded at Southampton, one passenger asked a deck hand:
'Is this ship really non-sinkable?'
'Yes, lady,' he replied. 'God Himself could not sink this ship.'

In 1997, Film Director James Cameron made what has been described as 'the most expensive movie ever made', starring Kate Winslet and Leonardo DiCaprio. In the passage which follows, James Cameron talks about his thoughts on the *Titanic* and the challenge of making a film about it.

Titanic still captures our imaginations after eighty-five years because her story is like a great novel that really happened. The story could not have been written better . . . the juxtaposition[1] of rich and poor, the gender roles played out unto death (women first), the stoicism[2] and nobility of a bygone age, the

5 magnificence of the great ship matched in scale only by the folly of the men who drove her hell-bent through the darkness. And above all the lesson: that life is uncertain, the future unknowable . . . the unthinkable possible.

The tragedy has assumed an almost mythic quality in our collective imagination, but the passage of time has robbed it of its human face. Its status

10 in our culture has become that of a morality tale referred to more often as a metaphor in political cartoons than as an actual event. I set out to make a film that would bring the event to life, to humanise it; not a docudrama, but an experience in living history. I wanted to place the audience on the ship, in its final hours, to live out the tragic event in all its horribly fascinating glory.

15 The greatest challenge of writing a new film about such an oft-told subject is the very fact that the story is so well known. What to say that hasn't been said? The only territory I felt had been left unexplored in prior films was the territory of the heart. I wanted the audience to cry for *Titanic*. Which means to cry for the *people* on the ship, which really means to cry for any lost soul in their hour

20 of untimely death. But the deaths of 1,500 innocents is too abstract for our hearts to grasp, although the mind can form the number easily.

To fully experience the tragedy of *Titanic*, to be able to comprehend it in human terms, it seemed necessary to create an emotional lightning rod for the audience by giving them two main characters they care about and then taking

25 those characters into hell.

Jack and Rose were born out of this need and the story of *Titanic* became their story. I realised that my film must be, first and always, a love story.

The story of *Titanic* and her fate seemed a magnificent canvas on which to paint a love story, a canvas offering the full spectral range of human emotion.

30 The greatest of loves can only be measured against the greatest of adversities, and the greatest of sacrifices thus defined. *Titanic* in all her terrible majesty provides this as does no other historical event.

© James Cameron

[1] *juxtaposition*: placing side by side.

[2] *stoicism*: the quality of showing great self-control and bravery when faced with difficulties.

QUESTIONS

The questions which follow are designed to help you explain your understanding of what you have just read. Sometimes this can be done by asking you to quote the author's actual words and sometimes by asking you to explain his point in your own words. This is clearly indicated in each question.

1. James Cameron thinks of the story of *Titanic* as 'a great novel that really happened'.

    (a) QUOTE two of the themes of the film that you might also expect to find in a classic novel. (*2 marks*)

    (b) IN YOUR OWN WORDS explain what one of these themes consists of. (*1 mark*)

2. IN YOUR OWN WORDS explain what Cameron sees as the lesson or moral of the story. (*1 mark*)

3. What was James Cameron aiming to achieve in his retelling of the story? (QUOTE) (*1 mark*)

4. What did he think was the greatest difficulty facing him? (QUOTE) (*1 mark*)

5. 'The deaths of 1,500 innocents is too abstract for our hearts to grasp.' (line 20). IN YOUR OWN WORDS, explain what you think he means by this statement. (*2 marks*)

6. IN YOUR OWN WORDS, describe his solution to the problem of 'humanising' the story. (*2 marks*)

7. (a) QUOTE a metaphor which describes the role of the characters of Jack and Rose. (*1 mark*)

    (b) IN YOUR OWN WORDS, say what you think the writer means by this metaphor. (*1 mark*)

Total: 12 marks

TITANIC (2): THE REVIEW

The following passage is a slightly condensed version of a review by Barbara Ellen which appeared in 'The Times' when the film was shown on television for the first time.

Things didn't augur well for James Cameron's 1997 blockbuster *Titanic* (BBC 1, Christmas Day, 5.45 pm), starring Kate Winslet and Leonardo DiCaprio. The 'most expensive movie ever made', coming in at a cool $200 million, was beset with well-publicised delays and technical problems — the ship wouldn't float or
5 sink on command; the sea wouldn't thrash; presumably Winslet's voice was more masculine than DiCaprio's.

When, finally, the film was released, everything was set for *Titanic* to become an embarrassing flop. Instead, it became a huge hit, making stars of Winslet and DiCaprio, and proving that there's nothing cinema audiences like better
10 than a good cry followed by a good snog. For, as well as being a blockbuster, *Titanic* is a date movie.

Pretty people in peril have always paid dividends at the box office, and few people come prettier than Winslet and DiCaprio, and few situations are more perilous than an iceberg spearing a vessel carrying over 2,000 passengers in
15 1912.

Just in case audiences get restless with the historical emphasis, Cameron also employs the dramatic device of a present-day diving team, hired to find a priceless diamond which went down with the ship. Instead, they unearth a painting of a beautiful young woman. Then 101-year old Rose comes forward to
20 tell her story and, disbelief rather generously suspended by the audience, it's time to sit back and enjoy the yarn.

All disaster movies have a love story and with *Titanic* we get Winslet's spoilt American socialite Rose being pursued by DiCaprio's poor, charming artist under the nose of her caddish millionaire fiancé (Billy Zane in cartoon villain
25 mode).

Both leads are engaging and confident, even though it is difficult to buy the idea of boyish DiCaprio and womanly Winslet as a couple — they look positively ludicrous together, about as compatible as Laurel and Hardy.

The real star, of course, is the ship. No one is ever going to watch a movie called
30 *Titanic* and expect a twist-in-the-tale ending. However, Cameron manages to imbue the inevitability of the climax with enough human interest and visual sparks to keep you interested. Some might scoff at the image of Winslet with her arms outstretched at the front of the ship, but *Titanic* is not a documentary; it is a movie. Bar all the death and drowning, it's perfect family viewing for Christmas
35 Day.

QUESTIONS

1. What, according to the reviewer, might have led us to expect that the film would not be a success? *(3 marks)*

2. Basing your answer on the third paragraph, explain what made the film such a hit. *(2 marks)*

3. Which aspect of the film does the reviewer criticise? *(2 marks)*

4. This passage is in many ways written in a style which is typical of film reviews.

    (a) QUOTE a phrase, line or sentence that suggests this. *(1 mark)*

    (b) QUOTE from the passage to show that the reviewer occasionally adopts a critical or sarcastic tone. *(1 mark)*

    (c) QUOTE from the passage to show that the reviewer is generally positive about the film. *(1 mark)*

    Total: 10 marks

WRITING ASSIGNMENTS

These could be done as homework exercises.

1. Compare the two passages on the 'Titanic' film. Write an essay in which you consider the following:

    ◆ points on which both the reviewer and director would agree;
    ◆ points in the review which it is likely that the director James Cameron would NOT agree with;
    ◆ any similarities or differences in the use of language between the two passages. For help, look at *(a)* the list of literary terms and figures of speech on pages 11–15 and *(b)* your answers to the shorter questions on each passage above. You can work some of these points into your essay.

2. Imagine you are James Cameron (the director). Using a first person style, write a letter to Barbara Ellen (the reviewer) responding to her published review of the film.

    OR

3. Imagine you are Barbara Ellen (the reviewer). Write a letter to James Cameron telling him about your view of the film.

Suggestions . . .

- Use a first person style ('I').
- You can adopt either a serious, factual approach or a more light-hearted, personal one.
- Remember to divide your essay into paragraphs, and to check spelling and punctuation.
- If you have seen the film, you can draw on your own knowledge. If not, simply pick up and expand upon some of the points made in the above two extracts.

DETECTIVES (1): SHERLOCK HOLMES

The famous detective Sherlock Holmes was a creation of Sir Arthur Conan Doyle. In this extract adapted from 'A Study in Scarlet' (1887), a puzzled police officer, Inspector Gregson, has called in Holmes for a second opinion on a murder. The person narrating the story is Holmes' friend, Dr. Watson.

'You will have your data soon,' I remarked, pointing with my finger; 'this is the Brixton Road, and that is the house, if I am not very much mistaken.'

'So it is. Stop, driver, stop!' We were still a hundred yards or so from it, but he insisted upon our alighting, and we finished our journey upon foot.

5 Number 3, Lauriston Gardens, wore an ill-omened look. It was one of four which stood back some little way from the street, two being occupied and two empty. The latter looked out with three tiers of vacant melancholy windows, which were blank and dreary, except that here and there a 'To Let' card had developed like a cataract upon the bleared panes. A small garden sprinkled over with a scattered
10 eruption of sickly plants separated each of these houses from the street and was traversed by a narrow pathway, yellowish in colour, and consisting apparently of a mixture of clay and gravel. The whole place was very sloppy from the rain which had fallen through the night. The garden was bounded by a three-foot brick wall with a fringe of wood rails upon the top, and against this
15 wall was leaning a stalwart police constable, surrounded by a small knot of loafers, who craned their necks and strained their eyes in the vain hope of catching some glimpse of the proceedings within.

I had imagined that Sherlock Holmes would at once have hurried into the house and plunged into a study of the mystery. Nothing appeared to be further from his
20 intention. For some reason, he lounged up and down the pavement, and gazed vacantly at the ground, the sky, the opposite houses and the line of railings.

Having finished his scrutiny, he proceeded slowly down the path, or rather down the fringe of grass which flanked the path,
25 keeping his eyes riveted upon the ground. Twice he stopped, and once I saw him smile, and heard him utter an exclamation of satisfaction. There were many marks of footsteps upon the wet, clayey soil; but since
30 the police had been coming and going over it, I was unable to see how my companion could hope to learn anything from it. Still, I had had such extraordinary evidence of the quickness of his perceptive faculties, that I had no doubt that he could see a great deal which was hidden from me.

At the door of the house we were met by a tall, white-faced, flaxen-haired man,
35 with a notebook in his hand, who rushed forward and wrung my companion's hand. 'It is indeed kind of you to come,' he said. 'I have had everything left untouched.'

'Except that!' my friend answered, pointing at the pathway. 'If a herd of buffaloes had passed along there could not be a greater mess. No doubt, however, you
40 had drawn your own conclusions, Gregson, before you permitted this.'

QUESTIONS

1. Look at Dr Watson's opening comment in line 1. What do you imagine Sherlock Holmes had said just before this? (2)

2. A hundred yards from the house, Holmes 'insisted upon our alighting, and we finished our journey upon foot.' Why do you think he did this? (2)

3. Explain what the writer means when he says that the house had an 'ill-omened look' (line 5). (2)

4. The dictionary defines the word 'cataract' (line 9) as follows:

   an eye condition which causes the lens to become opaque and unable to reflect light.

   (a) What figure of speech is the writer using when he says "here and there a 'To Let' card had developed like a cataract upon the bleared panes"? (1)

   (b) Explain why the author uses the word 'cataract' here. (2)

5. **In your own words**, describe the features of the garden that were particularly unattractive. (3)

6. Quote the phrase which tells us that the onlookers were not likely to see what was going on inside the house. (1)

7. **In your own words**, explain *(a)* what the narrator thought Sherlock Holmes would do and *(b)* what he did in fact do. (4)

8. Explain in your own words: *the quickness of his perceptive faculties* (line 32). (2)

9. The narrator of the passage is Dr. Watson, Holmes' friend.

    (a) Quote a phrase which shows his admiration of Holmes' skill. (1)

    (b) Quote another phrase in which Watson suggests some criticism of him. (1)

10. Why was Holmes annoyed when he met Inspector Gregson? (2)

11. Comment on the tone of Holmes' last remark:
    No doubt, however, you had drawn your own conclusions, Gregson, before you permitted this. (2)

    Total Marks: 25

DETECTIVES (2): INSPECTOR REBUS

Ian Rankin is a modern crime writer whose Inspector Rebus books are set in Edinburgh. In this extract from 'Dead Souls' (1999), Rebus is investigating the mysterious death of another police officer, Jim Margolies.

He stood atop Salisbury Crags. There was a fierce wind blowing, and he turned up the collar of his coat. He'd been home to change out of his funeral clothes and should have been heading back for the station — he could see St Leonard's from here — but something had made him take this detour.

5 Behind and above him, a few hardy souls had achieved the summit of Arthur's Seat. Their reward: the panoramic view, plus ears that would sting for hours. With his fear of heights, Rebus didn't get too close to the edge. The landscape was extraordinary. It was as though God had slapped his hand down on to Holyrood Park, flattening part of it but leaving this sheer face of rock, a reminder

10 of the city's origins.

Jim Margolies had jumped from here. Or a sudden gust had taken him: that was the less plausible, but more easily digested alternative. His widow had stated her belief that he'd been 'walking, just walking', and had lost his footing in the dark. But this raised unanswerable questions. What would take him from his
15 bed in the middle of the night? If he had worries, why did he need to think them out at the top of Salisbury Crags, several miles from his home? He lived in The Grange, in what had been his wife's parents' house. It was raining that night, yet he didn't take the car. Would a desperate man notice he was getting soaked . . . ?

20 Looking down, Rebus saw the site of the old brewery, where they were going to build the new Scottish parliament. The first in three hundred years, and sited next to a theme park. Nearby stood the Greenfield housing scheme, a compact maze of high-rise blocks and sheltered accommodation. He wondered why the Crags should be so much more impressive than the man-made
25 ingenuity of high-rises, then reached into his pocket for a folded piece of paper. He checked an address, looked back down on to Greenfield, and knew he had one more detour to make.

Greenfield's flat-roofed tower blocks had been built in the mid-1960s and were showing their age. Dark stains bloomed on the discoloured harling[1]. Overflow
30 pipes dripped water on to cracked paving slabs. Rotting wood was flaking from the window surrounds. The wall of one ground-floor flat, its windows boarded up, had been painted to identify the one-time tenant as 'Junky Scum'.

No council planner had ever lived here. No director of housing or community architect. All the council had done was move in problem tenants and tell
35 everyone central heating was on its way. The estate had been built on the flat bottom of a bowl of land, so that Salisbury Crags loomed monstrously over the whole. Rebus rechecked the address on the paper. He'd had dealings in Greenfield before. It was far from the worst of the city's estates, but still had its troubles. It was early afternoon now, and the streets were quiet. Someone had
40 left a bicycle, missing its front wheel, in the middle of the road. Further along stood a pair of shopping trolleys, nose to nose as though deep in local gossip. In the midst of the six eleven-storey blocks stood four neat rows of terraced
45 bungalows, complete with pocket-handkerchief gardens and low wooden fences. Net curtains covered most of the windows, and above each door a burglar alarm had been secured to the wall.

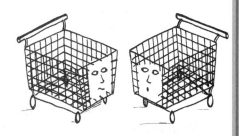

50 Part of the tarmac arena between the tower blocks had been given over to a play area. One boy was pulling another along on a sledge, imagining snow as the runners scraped along the ground. Rebus called out the words 'Cragside Court' and the boy on the sledge waved in the direction of one of the blocks.

55 When Rebus got up close to it, he saw that a sign on the wall identifying the building had been defaced so that 'Cragside' read 'Crap-site'. A window on the second floor swung open.

'You needn't bother,' a woman's voice boomed. 'He's not here.'

Rebus stood back and angled his head upwards.

60 'Who is it I'm supposed to be looking for?'

'Trying to be smart?'

'No, I just didn't know there was a clairvoyant on the premises. Is it your husband or your boyfriend I'm after?'

The woman stared down at him, made up her mind that she'd spoken too soon.

65 'Never mind', she said, pulling her head back and closing the window.

There was an intercom system, but only the numbers of flats, no names. He pulled at the door; it was unlocked anyway. He waited a couple of minutes for the lift to come, then let it shudder its way slowly up to the fifth floor. A walkway, open to the elements, led him past the front doors of half a dozen flats until he

70 was standing outside 5/14 Cragside Court. There was a window, but curtained with what looked like a frayed blue bedsheet. The doors showed signs of abuse: failed break-ins maybe, or just people kicking at it because there was no bell or knocker. No nameplate, but that didn't matter. Rebus knew who lived here.

75 Darren Rough.

© Ian Rankin

[1]harling: material used on the outer surface of a building
                 and containing small pieces of gravel.

QUESTIONS

1. Look at the opening paragraph. Quote **two** phrases which show that Inspector Rebus had not intended to go to Salisbury Crags.   (2)

2. What did Rebus (a) like and (b) dislike about being there?   (2)

3. What **two** possible explanations are put forward for the death of Jim Margolies? (2)

4. What **three** objections were there to the second explanation? (3)

5. Comment on the sentence in lines 21–22 describing the new Scottish Parliament building. *'The first in three hundred years, and sited next to a theme park.'* (2)

6. Describe in your own words the condition of the Greenfield tower blocks. (2)

7. What is ironic about the name of the housing estate? (2)

8. *'No council planner had ever lived here. No director of housing or community architect'* (line 33). What criticism of these people is implied here? (2)

9. Why does Rankin draw attention to the net curtains and burglar alarms on the bungalows? (2)

10. What impression do we gain of Inspector Rebus from his conversation with the woman at the window? Back up your answer with evidence. (2)

11. Comment on the effectiveness of the imagery in the sentence: *'Further along stood a pair of shopping trolleys, nose to nose as though deep in local gossip'* (lines 40–42). (2)

12. Comment on any aspect of the paragraph or sentence structures used in this passage. (2)

Total Marks 25

WRITING ASSIGNMENT

Write an essay comparing these two passages. You might consider the similarities and differences between the following:

♦ The period in which each story is set.
♦ The kind of area in which the story is set.
♦ The personalities of the two detectives.
♦ The approach taken by the narrator.
♦ The use of language devices (such as figures of speech and other methods of description, word choice, direct speech, sentence and paragraph structure, etc.).
♦ Any other ideas of your own.

JOURNALISM (1): THE CAT CAME BACK

Photograph by permission of Jaguar Cars Ltd.

In this article from 'The Herald', journalist Dominic Ryan describes his reactions to driving the Jaguar S-Type for the first time.

Not since the day I was persuaded by a hairdresser to dye my hair with industrial bleach has my appearance on the streets turned so many heads. Only this time there are slack-jawed looks of admiration rather than mirth.

5　I can see the words forming — "That's the new Jag!" — as I slide by in a ship so white it could outdazzle Liberace's teeth, yet is as subtle and refined in form as a gentleman's agreement.

This, ladeez and gentlemen, is the Jaguar S-Type. It is, beyond doubt, the shape of things to come with a more gracious nod in the direction of splendour past.

10　I'm told by those whose barnets have whitened not with peroxide but the onset of mid-life winter that once upon a time the Mark II Jaguar was king of the road and that this pretender owes its heritage to that traditional form.

Certainly, the front end is a supreme example of retro-look styling, with beautifully curving wings and flared wheel arches moulding themselves into the twin headlamps, all centred on a smooth, perfectly formed air-intake grille and topped off by an indisputable Top Cat badge (in America they've been allowed to retain the leaping Jaguar, quintessential sign of grace and power; here we must abide by the Euro pedestrian-protection rule).

Inside, the wood inserts in the dashboard blend well with the matt plastic. Cup-holders, ubiquitous in all modern vehicles (can we really not go between stops without an infusion of sugary water?), are, at least, discreet, hidden under the central arm rest.

Not quite so discreet is the audio-cassette holder next to the hi-fi controls. Emblazoned on its front is the roaring head of a wild cat which resembles not so much an Amazonian royal but flashing insignia from an arcade pinball machine.

But what of performance? When a car looks this good, does it matter? Of course, it must, or we'd all be wheeling around on Rollerblades and Armani jump suits.

Well, the news is good. Supreme looks are matched by exquisitely refined mechanics.

There's more energy expended flicking a Subbuteo player than changing gear and take-off is sudden, swift and smoother than a penguin's belly on ice.

The instant power injection is thanks to the gargantuan 3-litre AJ-V6 engine which delivers oodles of torque.

But more important than numbers, when the tough gets going, the engine doesn't purr like a kitten: it growls like an alley cat — a rich, vibrant sound in a cabin where there's only a hint of a hiss of road noise even at high speed.

Ah, the S-Type. Travelling in style, guvnor.

If the Ford Mondeo were a woman it might be Anthea Turner: not too painful to look at and a good performer in an undemanding medium. The Jaguar S-Type, on the other hand, would be vintage Honor Blackman: curves, grace, and growls, all dressed up in a figure-hugging cat suit.

Miaow!

QUESTIONS

1. In the writer's view, which features of the car point 'in the direction of splendour past'? (2)

2. State one feature of the car of which the writer is critical. (1)

3. Write down three FACTS about the car that the writer tells us. (3)

4. Quote two OPINIONS about the car that he expresses. (2)

5. (i) One aspect of the writer's style is that he sometimes expresses himself in a long-winded way to achieve a humorous effect. What, in simple terms, does he mean by *those whose barnets have whitened not with peroxide but the onset of mid-life winter* (lines 10–11)? (2)

    (ii) Another aspect of his style is that he sometimes uses a spoken rather than written style of expression. Find an example and try to suggest a reason why he does this. (2)

6. (i) This passage employs a variety of different registers [see pages 11–15]. Quote an example of:
    (a) jargon;
    (b) colloquial language;
    (c) formal language;
    (d) hyperbole. (4)

    (ii) Choose one of the examples you quoted above and explain what effect the author was aiming at and why you found this effective. (2)

7. (i) The writer also uses many comparisons. Quote an example of:
    (a) a simile;
    (b) a metaphor. (2)

    (ii) In one of the examples you have chosen, state what is compared to what and explain why you find the comparison effective. (2)

8. The name of the Jaguar car is, of course, taken from that of the animal which is a member of the cat family. Explain how the writer develops this basic comparison between the car and the cat in the course of the whole passage. (3)

Total Marks: 25

JOURNALISM (2):
'A SUDDEN, SERIOUS BRUSH WITH MORTALITY'

In this passage, Sandy Strang reflects on the dangers of Formula 1 motor racing and on racing driver David Coulthard's recent escape from a serious aircraft accident.

The enduring appeal of sport, said Hugh McIlvanney once, is that, at its best, it can offer a form of pure truth often absent in real life. Reality is generally messy, random, unstructured, but sport's disciplined formats can provide a marvellous forum for some of the great life-enhancing abstractions — courage, endeavour,
5   beauty — to flourish in a thrilling and compelling light.

In the end, though, in essence it matters little. For all the riveting seriousness with which practitioners and fans embrace their sporting obsessions, sport is essentially a frivolity. An arresting celebration of life it can be, but it is not, and can never aspire to be, a legitimate substitute for reality.

10   Who better to judge such truths than those supreme sportsmen, seemingly immortal and sacrosanct, who have experienced a sudden, serious brush with mortality? Men who thereby acquire an especial, privileged focus that what really matters is not sport, but life itself. Formula One motor racing intrinsically invites taboo thoughts of death. 'I am indeed a believer', Alain Prost
15   once admitted, 'but at the start of a Grand Prix with 156 litres of fuel behind me, I don't entirely rely on God. I rely on Prost to negotiate the first bend — and then the rest of it.'

David Coulthard has been there. Professional life of late had been unremittingly grim, bedevilled
20   by the doubts of others, and, one suspects, himself too, about his temperament and tenacity, and plagued by an epic run of bad luck with technical gremlins. Then, last month
25   brought a harrowing rendezvous with the

grim reaper. Two men lost their lives in a light aircraft crash; three cracked ribs for DC was a relatively minor inconvenience. His composed, dignified deportment as he visibly grew in the harrowing aftermath was genuinely
30 inspirational. Surviving the essence of scary had liberated him.

Further rejuvenated by earlier top podium slots at Silverstone, Spa and Monza, Coulthard journeyed to that most glamorously romantic of all stages on the F1 Circuit at Monte Carlo. That gloriously treacherous street drive once defined by Graham Hill as like balancing an egg on a spoon while shooting the rapids.
35 Coulthard handled the Mercedes McLaren like she was painted to the road, and became the first British driver to win there since fellow Scot Jackie Stewart twenty-seven years previously. Just as significantly, he did so in glorious style.

He was a revelation not only to a worldwide audience but, one fancies, to himself too. The crippling ghosts of self-doubt were ruthlessly exorcised. From
40 a fortuitous scrape with death, Coulthard has emerged reinvigorated and tougher.

Calamity has been his true touchstone. Equally admirably, whatever his success, like Stewart he won't need a bigger size in helmets.

QUESTIONS

1. Explain one way in which the opening paragraph suggests that sport can be better than real life. (2)

2. Quote one word used to describe sport in paragraph two that contradicts this view. (1)

3. Explain in your own words: *a sudden, serious brush with mortality* (lines 11–12). (2)

4. How does an experience such as this change someone's view of sport? (2)

The answers to questions 5 to 8 are all to be found in paragraph four (lines 18–30).

5. For David Coulthard *professional life of late had been unremittingly grim.* (lines 18–19).
    Write down three of the difficulties he had faced before the accident. (3)

6. Quote an example of personification. (1)

7. In what way was David Coulthard fortunate in the air crash? (2)

8. Quote two separate words or phrases that show that the author admires David Coulthard's behaviour after the crash. (2)

9. Graham Hill (a well-known racing driver from the 1960s) is quoted as describing the Formula One race at Monte Carlo as being 'like balancing an egg on a spoon while shooting the rapids' (line 34).

   (a) What figure of speech is he using here? (1)

   (b) What do you think he means by this comparison? (2)

10. Quote an expression from paragraph five which describes Coulthard's skill as a racing driver. (1)

11. Re-read lines 38–41.
    In your own words, explain **one** of the ways in which David Coulthard has gained from his recent difficult experiences. (2)

12. *He won't need a bigger size in helmets* (line 43).
    What point is being made here? (2)

13. Find a word in the passage that corresponds to each of the following meanings:
    (a) to be given new life and energy;
    (b) forbidden. (2)

Total marks: 25

WRITING ASSIGNMENT

Write an essay comparing these two passages of journalism. You might consider the similarities and differences between the following:

♦   the way the writers combine factual information and personal opinion;
♦   the use of both formal and informal language;
♦   word choice, sentence structure, figures of speech and other aspects of written language.

Remember to back up your points by quoting examples from both extracts.

FANTASY (1): THE HOWLER

This extract from J.K. Rowling's 'Harry Potter and the Chamber of Secrets' describes an unusual way of delivering a message.

The next day, however, Harry barely grinned once. Things started to go downhill from breakfast in the Great Hall. The four long house tables were laden with tureens of porridge, plates of kippers, mountains of toast and
5   dishes of eggs and bacon, beneath the enchanted ceiling (today, a dull cloudy grey). Harry and Ron sat down at the Gryffindor table next to Hermione, who had her copy of *Voyages with Vampires* propped open against a milk jug. There was a slight stiffness in the way she said 'Morning'
10   which told Harry that she was still disapproving of the way they had arrived. Neville Longbottom, on the other hand, greeted them cheerfully. Neville was a round-faced and accident-prone boy with the worst memory of anyone Harry had ever met.

15   'Post's due any minute — I think Gran's sending on a few things I forgot.'

Harry had only just started his porridge when, sure enough, there was a rushing sound overhead and a hundred or so owls streamed in, circling the Hall and dropping letters and packages into the chattering crowd. A big, lumpy parcel
20   bounced off Neville's head, and a second later, something large and grey fell into Hermione's jug, spraying them all with milk and feathers.

'Errol !' said Ron, pulling the bedraggled owl out by the feet. Errol slumped, unconscious, onto the table, his legs in the air and a damp red envelope in his beak.

25   'Oh no —' Ron gasped.

'It's all right, he's still alive,' said Hermione, prodding Errol gently with the tip of her finger.

'It's not that — it's *that*.'

Ron was pointing at the red envelope. It looked quite ordinary to Harry, but Ron
30   and Neville were both looking at it as though they expected it to explode.

'What's the matter?' said Harry.

'She's — she's sent me a Howler,' said Ron faintly.

'You'd better open it, Ron,' said Neville, in a timid whisper. 'It'll be worse if you don't. My Gran sent me one once, and I ignored it and —' he gulped, 'it was
35   horrible.'

Harry looked from their petrified faces to the red envelope.

'What's a Howler?' he said.

But Ron's whole attention was fixed on the letter, which had begun to smoke at the corners.

40 'Open it,' Neville urged. 'It'll all be over in a few minutes ...'

Ron stretched out a shaking hand, eased the envelope from Errol's beak and slit it open. Neville stuffed his fingers in his ears. A split second later, Harry knew why. He thought for a moment it *had* exploded; a roar of sound filled the huge Hall, shaking dust from the ceiling.

45 *'... STEALING THE CAR, I WOULDN'T HAVE BEEN SURPRISED IF THEY'D EXPELLED YOU, YOU WAIT TILL I GET HOLD OF YOU, I DON'T SUPPOSE YOU STOPPED TO THINK WHAT YOUR FATHER AND I WENT THROUGH WHEN WE SAW IT HAD GONE ...'*

Mrs. Weasley's yells, a hundred times louder than usual, made the plates and
50 spoons rattle on the table, and echoed deafeningly off the stone walls. People throughout the Hall were swivelling around to see who had received the Howler and Ron sank so low in his chair that only his crimson forehead could be seen.

*'... LETTER FROM DUMBLEDORE LAST NIGHT, I THOUGHT YOUR FATHER WOULD DIE OF SHAME, WE DIDN'T BRING YOU UP TO BEHAVE
55 LIKE THIS, YOU AND HARRY COULD BOTH HAVE DIED ...'*

Harry had been wondering when his name was going to crop up. He tried very hard to look as though he couldn't hear the voice that was making his eardrums
60 throb.

*'... ABSOLUTELY DISGUSTED, YOUR FATHER'S FACING AN INQUIRY AT WORK, IT'S ENTIRELY YOUR FAULT AND IF YOU PUT ANOTHER TOE OUT
65 OF LINE WE'LL BRING YOU STRAIGHT BACK HOME.'*

A ringing silence fell. The red envelope, which had dropped from Ron's hand, burst into flames and curled into ashes. Harry and Ron sat stunned, as though a tidal wave had just passed over them. A few people laughed and gradually, a
70 babble of talk broke out again.

QUESTIONS

1. What do you consider the properties of the 'enchanted ceiling' might have been? Refer to evidence from the passage that gives you a clue. (2)

2. In your own words, explain two characteristics of Neville Longbottom's personality. (2)

3. 'What's a Howler?' Harry asked the others. In the light of what happens in the course of the remainder of the passage, attempt to answer Harry's question. (2)

4. The Howler contains 'Mrs Weasley's yells, a hundred times louder than usual . . .' How does the author attempt to convey the tone of the spoken message in printed form? (1)

5. *(a)* Re-read the first extract from the message '. . . *STEALING THE CAR . . . HAD GONE . . .*' (lines 45–48). Comment on the punctuation of this extract. (1)

   (b) Suggest a reason why the author has punctuated the message in this way. (1)

   (c) Rewrite the extract with the correct punctuation. (2)

6. The message of Mrs Weasley's Howler contains emotive language (see page 13). Quote two examples of this kind of language from lines 45–66. (2)

7. The message is clearly meant as a reprimand to Ron and Harry.

   (a) Of what are they being accused? (1)

   (b) How had this been hinted at earlier in the passage? (Quote) (1)

   (c) In your own words, explain how (i) Ron and (ii) Harry reacted while the message was being heard. (4)

   (d) What is it that particularly seems to be upsetting Mrs Weasley? (2)

8. What is unusual about the expression 'ringing silence' (line 67)? What do you think the author meant by this? (2)

9. Good writers often use contrasting sentence lengths. For instance, they may suddenly put in a very short sentence to add to the feeling of drama or suspense. Find one place in the passage where J.K. Rowling does this. Suggest a reason why the short sentence is particularly suitable at this point. (2)

   Total marks: 25

FANTASY (2): IN THE RETIRING ROOM

The following passage is from the opening of 'Northern Lights' by Philip Pullman, a story set in an alternative world where every person is accompanied by a spirit in the form of an animal or bird, known as a daemon.

Lyra and her daemon moved through the darkening Hall, taking care to keep to one side, out of sight of the kitchen. The three great tables that ran the length of the Hall were laid already, the silver and the glass catching what little light there was, and the long benches were pulled out ready for the guests. Portraits of
5   former Masters hung high up in the gloom along the walls. Lyra reached the dais and looked back at the open kitchen door and, seeing no-one, stepped up beside the high table. The places here were laid with gold, or silver, and the fourteen seats were not oak benches but mahogany chairs with velvet cushions.

Lyra stopped beside the Master's chair and flicked the biggest glass gently with
10   a fingernail. The sound rang clearly through the Hall.

"You're not taking this seriously," whispered her daemon. "Behave yourself."

Her daemon's name was Pantalaimon, and he was currently in the form of a moth, a dark brown one so as not to show up in the darkness of the Hall.

"They're making too much noise to hear from the kitchen," Lyra whispered back.
15   "And the Steward doesn't come in till the first bell. Stop fussing."

But she put her palm over the ringing crystal anyway, and Pantalaimon fluttered ahead and through the slightly open door of the Retiring Room at the other end of the dais. After a moment he appeared again.

"There's no one there," he whispered. "But we must be quick".

20   Crouching behind the high table, Lyra darted along and through the door into the Retiring Room, where she stood up and looked around. The only light in here came from the fire-place, where a bright blaze of logs settled slightly as she looked, sending a fountain of sparks up into the chimney. She had lived most of her life in the College, but had never seen the Retiring Room before: only
25   Scholars and their guests were allowed in here, and never females. Even the maidservants didn't clean in here. That was the Butler's job alone.

Pantalaimon settled on her shoulder.

"Happy now? Can we go?" he whispered.

"Don't be silly! I want to look around!"

30   It was a large room, with an oval table of polished rosewood on which stood various decanters and glasses, and a silver smoking-mill with a rack of pipes.

"They do themselves well, don't they, Pan?" she said under her breath.

She sat in one of the green leather armchairs. "What d'you think they talk about?" Lyra said, or began to say, because before she finished the question
35   she heard voices outside the door.

"Behind the chair — quick!" whispered Pantalaimon, and in a flash Lyra was out of the armchair and crouching behind it. It wasn't the best one for hiding behind: she'd chosen one in the very centre of the
40 room and unless she kept very quiet . . .

The door opened, and the light changed in the room: one of the incomers was carrying a lamp, which he put down on the sideboard. Lyra could see his legs, in their dark green trousers and shiny
45 black shoes. It was a servant.

Then a deep voice said, "Has Lord Asriel arrived yet?"

It was the Master. As Lyra held her breath she saw the servant's daemon (a dog, like almost all servants' daemons) trot in and sit quietly at his feet, and then the Master's feet became visible too, in the shabby black shoes he always wore.

50 "No, master," said the Butler.

"I expect he'll be hungry when he arrives. Show him straight into Hall, will you?"

"Very good, Master."

"And you've decanted some of the special Tokay for him?"

"Yes, Master. The 1898, as you ordered. His Lordship's very partial to that, I
55 remember."

"Good. Now leave me, please."

The Butler bowed slightly and turned to leave, his daemon trotting obediently after him. From her not-much-of-a-hiding place Lyra watched as the Master went to a large oak wardrobe in the corner of the room, took his gown from a
60 hanger, and pulled it laboriously on. The Master had been a powerful man, but he was well over seventy now, and his movements were stiff and slow. The Master's daemon had the form of a raven, and as soon as his robe was on, she jumped down from the wardrobe and settled in her accustomed place on his right shoulder.

65 Lyra could feel Pantalaimon bristling with anxiety, though he made no sound. For herself, she was pleasantly excited. The visitor mentioned by the Master, Lord Asriel, was her uncle, a man whom she admired and feared greatly. He was fierce: if he caught her in here she'd be severely punished, but she could put up with that.

70 What she saw next, however, changed things completely.

The Master took from his pocket a folded paper and laid it on the table. He took the stopper out of the mouth of a decanter containing a rich golden wine, unfolded the paper, and poured a thin stream of white powder into the decanter before crumpling the paper and throwing it into the fire. Then he took a pencil
75 from his pocket and stirred the wine until the powder had dissolved, and replaced the stopper.

His daemon gave a soft brief squawk. The Master replied in an undertone, and looked around with his hooded, clouded eyes before leaving through the door he'd come in by.

80 Lyra whispered, "Did you see that, Pan?"

"Of course I did! Now hurry out, before the Steward comes!"

But as he spoke, there came the sound of a bell ringing once from the far end of the Hall.

"That's the Steward's bell!" exclaimed Lyra. "I thought we had more time than
85 that."

Pantalaimon fluttered swiftly to the Hall door, and swiftly back.

"The Steward's there already," he said. "And you can't get out of the other door . . ."

© Philip Pullman, 1998

QUESTIONS

1. Explain in your own words **two** pieces of evidence from the first paragraph (lines 1–8) which suggest Lyra is doing something she shouldn't. (2)

2. In line 1 the Hall is described as 'darkening'. Quote **two** words or phrases from the rest of the first paragraph which continue this idea. (1)

3. Give **two** reasons why you think the 'high table' (line 7) might be so called. (2)

4. Read lines 12–13, 'Her daemon's name . . . Hall'. Quote and explain the evidence which reveals that Pantalaimon can change his shape. (2)

5. 'a fountain of sparks' (line 23)
   (a) What figure of speech is used here? (1)
   (b) How does the expression help you picture the scene? (1)

6. Read lines 20–26. Explain in your own words **two** pieces of information which suggest the Retiring Room is a very special, exclusive place. (2)

7. (a) What is meant by 'They do themselves well' (line 32)? (1)
   (b) Explain in your own words how **two** of the examples from lines 30–31 help you to understand this. (2)

8. Explain the effect of the ellipsis [i.e., the three dots (. . .)] at the end of line 40. (2)

9. Suggest **one** reason why the author writes 'Then a deep voice said' rather than 'The Master said' in line 46. (1)

10. *(a)* Explain the word 'laboriously' (line 60). (1)

    (b) Show how the information given in the next sentence helps you understand this word. (2)

11. Read lines 71–76. What do you think the Master is doing here? (1)

12. Look again at lines 9–19, lines 27–29 and lines 65–69. Explain clearly the differences between Lyra's personality and Pantalaimon's which are revealed in these extracts. You should include some quotations from the extracts in your answer. (4)

Total Marks: 25

WRITING ASSIGNMENTS

1. Write an essay comparing the way in which each author captures your interest.

   You should consider:
   - how the personality of the main character (Lyra and Harry) is presented in each passage
   - how the authors combine realism with fantasy to make the fantasy elements more believable
   - how the two writers use language and presentation to create suspense
   - how each writer combines humour with suspense.

2. Write the opening chapter of a story with a fantasy theme. You should introduce one main character and a clear setting. You should also include one or two supernatural touches.

OR

3. Invent a character like Harry Potter or Lyra whom you imagine as the central figure in a fantasy book or books. Describe your character in detail.

CHILDHOOD IN FICTION (1): MAN AND BOY

In this extract from Tony Parsons' novel 'Man and Boy', the main character, Harry Silver, whose wife has left him to bring up their young son alone, describes Pat's first day at school.

Pat started school.

The uniform he had to wear should have made him look grown up. The grey V-necked sweater, the white shirt and yellow tie should
5 have made him look like a little man. But they didn't.

The formality of his school clothes only underlined the shocking newness of him. Approaching his fifth birthday, he wasn't even
10 young yet. He was still brand new. Even though he was dressed more grown-up than me.

As I helped him get ready for his first day at school, I was startled to realise just how much I loved his face. When he was a baby I couldn't
15 tell if he was really beautiful, or if that was just my parental software kicking in. But now I could see the truth.

With those light blue eyes, his long yellow hair and the way his slow, shy smile could spread right across his impossibly smooth face, he really was a beautiful
20 boy.

And now I had to let my beautiful boy go out into the world. At least until 3.30. For both of us, it felt like a lifetime.

He wasn't smiling now. At breakfast he was pale and silent in his pastiche of adult's clothing, struggling to stop his chin trembling and his bottom lip sticking
25 out, while over the Coco Pops I kept up a running commentary about the best days of your life.

Then it was time to go.

As we drove closer to the school I was seized by a moment of panic. There were children everywhere, swarms of them all in exactly the same clothes as Pat, all
30 heading in the same direction as us. I could lose him in here. I could lose him forever.

We pulled up some way from the school gates. There were cars double-parked and treble-parked everywhere. Tiny girls with Leonardo DiCaprio lunch boxes scrambled out of off-road vehicles the size of Panzer tanks. Bigger boys with

35 Arsenal and Manchester United kit-bags climbed out of old bangers. The noise from this three-foot-high tribe was unbelievable.

I took Pat's clammy hand and we joined the throng. I could see a collection of small, bewildered new kids and their nervous parents milling about in the playground. We were just going though the gates to join them when I noticed the

40 lace on one of Pat's brand new black leather shoes was undone.

'Let me get your lace for you, Pat,' I said, kneeling down to tie it, realising that this was the first day in his life he had ever been out of trainers.

Two bigger boys rolled past, arm in arm. They leered at us. Pat smiled at them shyly.

45 'He can't even do his shoes up,' one of them snorted.

'No,' Pat said, 'but I can tell the time.'

They collapsed in guffaws of laughter, holding each other up for support, and reeled away repeating what Pat had said with disbelief.

'But I can tell the time, can't I?' Pat said, thinking they doubted his word, his eyes

50 blinking furiously as he seriously considered bursting into tears.

'You can tell the time brilliantly,' I said, unable to really believe that I was actually going to turn my son loose among all the cynicism and spite of the lousy modern world. We went into the playground.

A lot of the children starting school had both parents with them. But I wasn't the

55 only lone parent. I wasn't even the only man.

The kindly headmistress came and led us into the assembly hall. She gave us a brief, breezy pep talk and then the children were all assigned to their individual classrooms.

Pat got Miss Waterhouse, and with a handful of other parents and new kids we

60 were marched off to her class by one of the trusted older children who were acting as guides. Our guide was a boy of around eight years old. Pat stared up at him, dumbstruck with admiration.

In Miss Waterhouse's class a flock of five-year-olds were sitting cross-legged on the floor, patiently waiting for a story from their teacher, a young woman with the

65 hysterical good humour of a game-show host.

'Welcome, everyone!' Miss Waterhouse said. 'You're just in time for our morning story. But first it's time for everyone to say goodbye to their mummy.' She beamed at me. 'And daddy.'

It was time to leave him. Although there had been a few emotional goodbyes before, this time felt a bit different. This time it felt as though I were being left.

He was starting school, and by the time he left school he would be a man and I would be middle-aged. Those long days of watching Star Wars videos at home while life went on somewhere else were over. Those days had seemed empty and frustrating at the time, but I missed them already. My baby was joining the world.

Miss Waterhouse asked for volunteers to look after the new boys and girls. A forest of hands shot up, and the teacher chose the chaperones. Suddenly a solemn, exceptionally pretty little girl was standing next to us.

'I'm Peggy,' she told Pat. 'And I'm going to take care of you.'

The little girl took his hand and led him into the classroom.

He didn't even notice me leaving.

© Tony Parsons

QUESTIONS

1. Read lines 1–11. 'Pat . . . more grown-up than me.'

    In your own words explain how Pat's uniform affected his appearance, and why this surprised his father, Harry.

    (2)

2. In lines 12–17, Harry wonders if his son is really as beautiful as he thinks. Explain the sentence 'When he was a baby . . . kicking in.' (lines 14–16)

    (2)

3. Look at lines 23–26. ('He wasn't smiling . . . your life'.)

    (a) **Quote two** separate words or short phrases which reveal Pat was nervous about starting school.

    (1)

    (b) Referring to the **same two** expressions, briefly suggest how you think Pat would usually appear or behave at breakfast.

    (2)

4. 'Then it was time to go.' (line 27)

   Suggest a reason why the writer puts this sentence in a paragraph by itself. (2)

5. Explain how the writer adds significantly to the meaning by his word choice of

   EITHER: 'swarms' (line 29)
   OR: 'tribe' (line 36) (2)

6. 'we were marched off to her class' (lines 59–60)

   Describe the tone of the word 'marched' and explain what it adds to the impression of the scene compared with a word such as 'taken'. (2)

7. (a) Why do you think the teacher just adds the words 'And daddy' as an afterthought? (line 68) (1)

   (b) Do you think the teacher adding the words 'And daddy' would make Harry feel better or worse about his situation as a single father? Explain why you think so. (1)

8. Look at lines 71–75. ('He was starting . . . joining the world'.)

   Explain in your own words one of the reasons mentioned why Harry feels sad about Pat starting school, making clear why it should make him sad. (2)

9. (a) What is the meaning of 'chaperones' in line 77? (1)

   (b) Pick out a piece of evidence from lines 76–80 (Miss Waterhouse . . . classroom) and explain how it helps you understand the meaning of 'chaperones'. (1)

10. 'He didn't even notice me leaving' (line 81).

    Explain **two** different emotions this fact might have aroused in Harry. (2)

11. In this account, the narrator, Harry, is shown to be very close to his son, Pat. Pick out **two** pieces of evidence from lines 28–39 (' As we drove . . . playground') and explain how each example reveals this closeness in their relationship. (4)

Total Marks: 25

CHILDHOOD IN FICTION (2): I KNOW THIS MUCH IS TRUE

The narrator of this extract, Dominick, is eight years old. His mother has taken him and his identical twin, Thomas, to the cinema. The year is 1958. The passage is taken from 'I Know This Much is True' by Wally Lamb.

Thomas and I are going to the movies with Ma — the Back-to-School Festival of Fun. We're on the city bus. I get to pull the stop cord when we get to the five-and-ten[1] because Thomas did it the last time. The bus won't stop at the show, only the five-and-ten.

5   We have the nice bus driver today — the one who says, "Hey, whaddaya got in there?" and pulls candy out of your ears. Last time we came downtown, we got the grouchy driver with no thumb. Ma thinks maybe he lost it in
10 the war or in a machine. She told me not to look at it if I was afraid of it, but I did look. I couldn't help it. I didn't want to but I did.

Here's the five-and-ten. Ma lifts me up and I pull the cord. "See you later, alligator!" the bus driver says when we get off. Ma smiles and Thomas says
15 nothing. From the safety of the sidewalk, I yell, "After a while, crocodile!" The driver laughs.

We walk over to the show. There's a line at the ticket booth. The kids right in front of us are big kids. Wiseguys. "Well, next time, bring your birth certificate then!" the ticket lady yells. It's the crippled lady. Sometimes she works inside at
20 the candy counter and sometimes she sells the tickets. Her and this other lady switch around. Ma says the crippled lady got polio before they had polio shots. Maybe that's why she's always crabby.

Inside, a bulgy-eyed man rips our tickets and gives Thomas and me our free back-to-school pencil boxes. With his pen, he makes an X on the back of our
25 hands. "One to a customer," he tells Ma. "I mark them so I can tell if some kid tries to pull a fast one."

I want to go all the way down in front, but Ma says no, it will hurt our eyes. She makes us stop halfway. Here's how we're sitting: first Thomas, then Ma, then me on the end. "Now, don't open your pencil boxes," Ma says.

30 The man in charge is called the husher. He has a uniform and a flashlight, and he's very, very tall. His job is to yell at kids when they put their feet on the seats in front of them. If they answer him back, he shines his flashlight right in their face.

35 They show cartoons first: Daffy Duck, Sylvester and Tweety, Road Runner. *Beep-beep! Beep-beep!* On the radio, they said, they were showing ten cartoons, but they don't. They show eight. I'm only on my eighth finger when the Three Stooges come on.

Ma doesn't like the Three Stooges. When Moe pokes his fingers in Larry's eyes, Ma leans over and whispers, "Don't you ever try anything like that now." Her
40 voice in my ear tickles — makes me scrunch up my shoulder. In this one, the three Stooges are bakers. They just finished decorating this fancy cake for a snotty rich lady, and she's yelling at them. Then Larry slips and falls back against Curly and Curly bumps into the rich lady and she falls right into the cake! All three of us laugh — Thomas and Ma and me.

45 There are lots of bad kids here with no mothers or fathers. They're talking loud and fooling around instead of watching the movie. "*I tawt I taw a puddy cat!*" one kid keeps yelling out, even though the cartoons are over. Every time he yells it, other kids laugh. Some boys in front have flattened their popcorn boxes and they're throwing them up in the air. The boxes make shadows on the screen.

50 "Can we get some popcorn?" I whisper to Ma.

"No," she whispers back.

"Why not?"

"Just watch the movie."

Thomas taps Ma's arm and I lean over to listen. "Ma, I'm thinking about her
55 again," he says. "What should I do?"

"Think about something else," she says. "Watch the movie."

Thomas means Miss Higgins. In just one more week, we'll be third-graders and Miss Higgins
60 will be our new teacher. She's the meanest teacher in our whole school. All summer long, Thomas has been getting stomach aches thinking about her.

Thomas opens his pencil box even
65 though we're not supposed to. He starts chewing on one of his brand-new pencils like it's corn on the cob.

I open my pencil box, too. If Thomas can, then so can I. I bend and bend my eraser to see how far I can bend it, and it boings out of my hand and into the 70 dark.

"See!' Ma says. "What did I tell you?" Down in front, someone yells a naughty word. Another kid screams. *Ping!* Something hits the back of my seat.

"Hey! Cut it out down there!" a voice yells. I look back. It's not the husher. It's Bulgy Eyes, the man who gave us our pencil boxes. Ma says those bad kids 75 better behave because he sounds like he really means business. She says Bulgy Eyes is the boss even though the husher is bigger. Now Thomas has his eraser in his mouth. He's sucking on it. *Slurp, slurp, slurp.* "What are you doing that for?" I say. He says he's cleaning it. Which is stupid. It's already clean. It's brand new.

80 The Three Stooges are over and Francis the Talking Mule comes on. *Francis goes to West Point.* Ma says West Point's a school . . . you know what? Last year, at our school, a dog snuck in. He came running into our classroom during spelling and knocked over the easel. All the kids were laughing and saying, "Here, boy!" and Miss Henault made us flip our spelling papers over and put our 85 heads on our desks to calm down. That dog came right up our row. He was tan and white and had a smiley face, and he smelled a little like a sewer. He had a collar on, though, so he must have belonged to somebody.

Ping! Ping! Ma says don't turn around or we might get hit in the eye. She says someone should complain to the manager before someone gets hurt. *Ping!* 90 We're cowboys. Bad guys are shooting at us. My new favourite cowboy show is *The Rifleman*. I used to like *Cheyenne* the best, but now I like *The Rifleman*.

I'm not really paying attention to this movie. I'm watching those bad kids instead — the ones up front. Popcorn boxes swoop in the dark like bats . . . sometimes bats come out on our street when it's getting dark. They look like birds but 95 they're not. They trick you. *Ping!* The lights come on even though the movie's still playing. "Hey!" everyone starts going. "Hey!" Then the movie stops.

Bulgy Eyes and the husher walk down the aisle and up on the stage, and Bulgy Eyes starts yelling at us. Ma's scared. Bulgy Eyes points his thumb at the husher. "You see this guy here? From now on, him and me are going to be 100 looking for troublemakers. And when we find 'em, we're going to kick 'em out and not give 'em their money back. And call their fathers. Understand?"

"Good," Ma whispers. "It serves them right."

Now everyone's real quiet. Just sitting there. The lights go off. The movie starts up. Bulgy Eyes and the husher walk up and down the aisles. All the bad kids are 105 being good.

© Wally Lamb

[1]Five-and-ten: shop where originally nothing cost more than fifteen cents

QUESTIONS

1. The 'Back-to-School Festival of Fun' (lines 1–2).

    Explain why the title of the picture show might seem ironic to children. (1)

2. Read lines 5–16. ('We have . . . the driver laughs.').

    Suggest in your own words **two** reasons why the children call one bus driver the 'nice' one. (2)

3. Read lines 17–22 ('We walk . . . crabby.')

    (a) Show how at least one piece of information in the paragraph helps you to understand the meaning of the word 'crabby' (line 22)? (2)

    (b) What other word used earlier in the passage has the same meaning as 'crabby'? (1)

4. Read lines 23–26. ("Inside, . . . a fast one.')

    Explain in your own words why the 'bulgy-eyed man' made an 'X' on the back of the boys' hands. (1)

5. Read lines 27–29 ('I want . . . on the end'.)

    Explain the choice of seats the narrator and his family make in the cinema. (2)

6. Explain the connection between 'I'm only on my eighth finger' (line 36) and the fact there are supposed to be ten cartoons on show. (2)

7. Read lines 38–44. ('Ma doesn't like . . . and me.')

    Why do you think the boys' mother disapproves of 'The Three Stooges'? (1)

8. Read lines 92–96. ("I'm not really . . . the movie stops.')

    (a) Explain the links in thought that lead the narrator from describing the behaviour of the 'bad kids' at the front of the cinema to a discussion on bats. (2)

    (b) Give another example from earlier in the passage of a similar jump in thought via a link. (1)

9. There are a number of expressions in italics in the passage (e.g., lines 35, 46, 72, 77, 80 / 81, 88, 91, etc.).

   Choose **two** of these examples which have a different reason for their use, and explain why the italics are used in each case. (2)

10. Compare the characters of the narrator and his identical twin, Thomas, as they are portrayed in this passage. Explain how far they seem alike in character and what sort of relationship they appear to have with each other. Support your answer with direct references and / or quotations. (4)

11. The narrator, Dominick, is an eight-year-old child. Explain how the writer gives the effect of a child describing events by discussing at least **two** examples of any **two** of the following:

   > sentence structure;
   > ideas;
   > word choice;
   > point of view / perspective;
   > descriptive language. (4)

Total Marks: 25

WRITING ASSIGNMENTS

1. Write an essay comparing the difference in the presentation of childhood in the two extracts, one being from an adult's point of view and the other from a child's point of view.

   You might include discussion of:

   ♦ how each writer presents the thoughts and feelings of the children;
   ♦ how each writer shows the relationships between children and adults;
   ♦ how each writer uses language to convey his ideas.

2. Think back to your early childhood.

   Write an account of your earliest memories of school.

   OR

   Write an account of a visit to a place of entertainment.

ADVICE ON TEXTUAL ANALYSIS (PRACTICAL CRITICISM)

'Textual Analysis' or 'Practical Criticism' are names given to the close study of short pieces of literature. The aim is to show your understanding of the texts and your appreciation of the techniques the writers have used. You will also be asked to consider how effectively the writer has achieved his or her purpose.

Getting started:

Step one:

Begin by reading the text. If it is a short text, you might read it more than once. You might skim-read it first, to get a general idea of what it is about, and then read it again.

Step two:

Read the text again more slowly, this time making notes on the page. This process is called **annotation**. You can make marginal notes on the ideas themselves, and also mark any pieces of expression that interest you: individual words or phrases; figures of speech; word order and so on. Don't just underline these — try to make a brief note of why you find something interesting. The following example will illustrate the kind of comments you could make.

CARGOES by John Masefield

Dictionary definition: ancient ship with five sets of oars. (Rowed by slaves — cruelty?)
Ancient times (Phoenician empire)

Quinquereme of Nineveh from distant Ophir

Rowing home to haven in sunny Palestine,

Exotic romantic places; alliteration and soft sounds in names appealing to ear

Steady, regular rhythm imitating oars

With a cargo of ivory,

Involve animals — hints of cruelty

And apes and peacocks,

Sandalwood, cedarwood, and sweet white wine.

Luxuries for rich: appeals to senses — smell, taste

Elizabethan age; elegant sailing ships: slow, dignified rhythm; exotic foreign locations

Stately Spanish galleon coming from the Isthmus,

Dipping through the Tropics by the palm-green shores,

Isthmus of Panama: Spanish have been raiding South America

Alliteration of 's' throughout verse suggests gentle splashing sound of sea on sailing ship

With a cargo of diamonds,

Emeralds, amethysts,

Gems beautiful toys for the rich: cinnamon a luxury

Topazes, and cinnamon, and gold moidores[1].

Many mono-syllables create punchy, jerky rhythm, full of energy; 'butting' suggests tough character

Dirty British coaster with a salt-caked smoke stack

Butting through the Channel in the mad March days,

Contrasts — ship dirty, not glamorous. Age of steam. Weather stormy

With a cargo of Tyne coal,

Ordinary useful things: exporting own products, not stealing or exploiting others

Road-rail, pig-lead,

Firewood, iron-ware, and cheap tin trays.

List of objects ends with comic anti-climax

Stanzas all have symmetrical structure which invites comparison

[1]old coins

Step three:

Unless you are working in examination conditions, you should now compare your annotations with those of others in your group or class and discuss your first impressions.

In the case of this text, for example, you might compare your responses to the last verse. How many of you see the dirty British ship as a come-down from the more elegant vessels of the past? Do others see it as having admirable qualities which the other two lack?

Since you have noticed the verses are structured symmetrically, what other comparisons are you prompted to make? (Think of techniques such as rhythm and sound as well as ideas.)

Once you have looked at the poem in detail, you might then consider what its deeper significance might be. Are the 'cargoes' symbolic in some way? Is the author suggesting we consider how civilisation has advanced over two thousand years or so?

PASSAGES FOR PRACTICE: POETRY

SNOW IN THE SUBURBS *by Thomas Hardy*

Every branch big with it,
Bent every twig with it;
Every fork like a white web-foot;
Every street and pavement mute:
5   Some flakes have lost their way, and grope back upward, when
Meeting those meandering down they turn and descend again.
The palings are glued together like a wall,
And there is no waft of wind with the fleecy fall.

A sparrow enters the tree,
10   Whereon immediately
A snow-lump thrice his own slight size
Descends on him and showers his head and eyes,
And overturns him,
And near inurns him,
15   And lights on a nether twig, when its brush
Starts off a volley of other lodging lumps with a rush.

The steps are a blanched slope,
Up which, with feeble hope,
A black cat comes, wide-eyed and thin;
20   And we take him in.

QUESTIONS

1.   Quote an example of *(a)* a simile and *(b)* a metaphor from the first verse. Comment on what is compared to what in each case, and why you consider the comparison to be effective. (4)

2.   Quote a word, phrase or line which conveys each of the following:
    (a) the heaviness of the snowfall;
    (b) the quietness of the scene. (2)

3.   What does the word 'meandering' suggest about the snow? (2)

4. 'waft of wind' (line 8).
   (a) What figure of speech is used here?
   (b) What point do you think the poet is trying to emphasise? (2)

5. In your own words, tell what happens to the sparrow in verse two. (4)

6. Explain two ways in which we might feel sorry for the cat. (2)

7. *Humour*
    Sympathy
    Pleasure
    Sadness
    Peacefulness
    . . . or something else?

   Which feelings do you find in this poem? (Back up your answer with evidence from the text). (4)

   Total Marks: 20

HAMNAVOE MARKET *by George Mackay Brown*

No school today! We drove in our gig to the town.
Grand-da bought us each a coloured balloon.
Mine was yellow, it hung high as the moon.
A cheapjack urged. Swingboats went up and down.

5   Coconuts, ice-cream, apples, ginger beer
Routed the five bright shillings in my pocket.
I won a bird-on-a-stick and a diamond locket.
The Blind Fiddler, the broken-nosed boxers were there.

The booths huddled like mushrooms along the pier.
10 I ogled a goldfish in its crystal cell.
Round every reeling corner came a drunk.

The sun whirled a golden hoof. It lingered. It fell
On a nest of flares. I yawned. Old Madge our mare
Homed through a night black as a bottle of ink.

QUESTIONS

1.   'No school today!' (line 1)
Explain how the exclamation mark helps us understand the tone of this
phrase. (Make clear what the tone is in your answer.)   (2)

2.   A 'gig' (line 1) is a small open horse-drawn cart. Pick out **two** other details
from the poem which suggest the setting is not in the present day.   (2)

3.   'Routed' (line 6) means 'completely defeated' or 'put to flight'.
Explain the sense in which the 'coconuts, ice cream, apples and ginger
beer' had 'routed' the shillings in the writer's pocket.   (2)

4.   'A diamond locket.' (line 7)
Why might the reader and the narrator of the poem picture this object
differently?   (2)

5.   'The booths huddled like mushrooms'. (line 9)
Explain **two** ways in which the booths might remind the writer of
mushrooms.   (2)

6. 'Reeling' (line 11) means staggering.
   Suggest a reason why the writer has placed it in front of 'corner' instead
   of in front of 'drunk'. (2)

7. Look at lines 12–13, 'The sun . . . yawned'.
   Show how the author uses sentence structure to suggest how the sun
   seemed to set gradually before darkness suddenly fell. (2)

8. Show how the writer's word choice presents an impression of colour and
   brightness in lines 1–13. (4)

9. Read lines 13–14, 'Old Madge . . . ink'.
   Explain how effective you find this sentence as an ending to the poem. (2)

Total Marks: 20

'OUT, OUT —' *by Robert Frost*

This poem is by the American writer, Robert Frost. It describes a fatal accident on a New England farm. A 'buzz' saw is a power-driven saw.

The buzz saw snarled and rattled in the yard
And made dust and dropped stove-length sticks of wood,
Sweet-scented stuff when the breeze drew across it.
And from there those that lifted eyes could count
5   Five mountain ranges one behind the other
Under the sunset far into Vermont.
And the saw snarled and rattled, snarled and rattled,
As it ran light, or had to bear a load.
And nothing happened: day was all but done.
10   Call it a day, I wish they might have said
To please the boy by giving him the half hour
That a boy counts so much when saved from work.
His sister stood beside them in her apron
To tell them 'Supper.' At the word, the saw,
15   As if to prove saws knew what supper meant,
Leaped out at the boy's hand, or seemed to leap —
He must have given the hand. However it was,
Neither refused the meeting. But the hand!
The boy's first outcry was a rueful laugh,
20   As he swung toward them holding up the hand,
Half in appeal, but half as if to keep
The life from spilling. Then the boy saw all —
Since he was old enough to know, big boy
Doing a man's work, though a child at heart —
25   He saw all spoiled. 'Don't let him cut my hand off —
The doctor, when he comes. Don't let him, sister!'
So. But the hand was gone already.
The doctor put him in the dark of ether.
He lay and puffed his lips out with his breath.
30   And then — the watcher at his pulse took fright.
No one believed. They listened at his heart.
Little — less — nothing! — and that ended it.
No more to build on there. And they, since they
Were not the one dead, turned to their affairs.

QUESTIONS

1. 'The buzz saw snarled and rattled in the yard.' (line 1)

   (a) Explain how the poet's word choice in this line conveys effectively the different sounds made by the saw. (2)

   (b) What is the saw being compared to with the use of the word 'snarled'? (1)

   (c) Suggest why the phrase 'snarled and rattled' is repeated twice more in line 7. (1)

2. 'And nothing happened'. (line 9)

   What is the effect of this sentence? (1)

3. What is the meaning of the expression 'Call it a day' (line 10)? (1)

4. Read lines 13–17, 'His sister . . . given the hand.'

   (a) In your own words, explain exactly why the accident occurred. (2)

   (b) Comment on the effectiveness of the expression 'As if to prove saws knew what supper meant'. (2)

5. Read lines 30–32, 'And then . . . ended it.'

   Show how the poet has used sentence structure and punctuation effectively to express the boy's last moments. (4)

6. Explain clearly the function and effect of the exclamation marks in line 18, 'But the hand!' and line 26, 'Don't let him, sister!' (4)

7. Read the last sentence, 'And they . . . their affairs.' (lines 33–34)

   Describe the poet's tone in this sentence. What thoughts and feelings do you think the poet has about people simply returning to work after the boy's death? (2)

Total Marks: 20

POEM FOR MY SISTER *by Liz Lochhead*

My little sister likes to try my shoes,
to strut in them,
admire her spindle-thin twelve-year-old legs
in this season's styles.
5   She says they fit her perfectly,
but wobbles
on their high heels, they're
hard to balance.

I like to watch my little sister
10 playing hopscotch, admire the neat hops-and-skips of her,
their quick peck,
never-missing their mark, not
over-stepping the line.
She is competent at peever[1].

15 I try to warn my little sister
about unsuitable shoes,
point out my own distorted feet, the callouses,
odd patches of hard skin.
I should not like to see her
20 in my shoes.
I wish she would stay
sure footed,
          sensibly shod.

[1]peever: a name used in some parts of Scotland for the children's game of hopscotch.

QUESTIONS

[The questions for this poem and the one which follows are laid out verse by verse. These questions are also slightly more detailed, totalling 25 marks]

Read Verse 1

1. Suggest **one** reason why a 'little sister' might try on a big sister's shoes.   (1)

2. Explain clearly what 'strut' (line 2) suggests about the way the little sister walks in her sister's shoes.   (2)

3. 'She says they fit her perfectly' (line 5)
Why do you think the poet adds the words 'she says'?   (1)

4. Pick out **one** word or phrase from verse 1 which you feel creates a comical picture and explain why you find it funny.   (2)

5. 'I like to watch . . . over-stepping the line.' (lines 9–13)
   Show how the poet uses sentence structure, rhythm and punctuation in
   these lines to suggest a game of hopscotch. (3)

6. Pick out **two** words from verse 2 which show the 'little sister' is an expert
   at her games. (2)

7. Compare the opening line of verse 3 (line 15) with the opening line of
   verse 2 (line 9).
   Explain how the poet's tone changes to show a different attitude to her
   sister. Make clear what her tone and attitude are in each of these lines. (3)

8. Explain in your own words **two** of the bad effects of wearing 'unsuitable
   shoes'. (2)

9. The phrase 'in my shoes' can mean literally wearing shoes. What other
   meaning can it have? (1)

10. The last verse of the poem can be seen as an extended metaphor, in
    which the poet is saying that she wishes to protect her sister from some
    of the harmful and painful experiences of life.
    Keeping this in mind, explain the metaphorical sense of any **two** of the
    following:
    'unsuitable shoes' (line 16)
    'my own distorted feet, the callouses, / odd patches of hard skin'
    (lines 17–18)
    'surefooted' (line 22)
    'sensibly shod' (line 23). (4)

11. Referring closely to the poem and using quotation, describe the
    relationship of the sisters as it is revealed in the poem. (4)

Total Marks: 25

HEATHER ALE *by Robert Louis Stevenson*

I

From the bonny bells of heather
They brewed a drink lang-syne,[1]
Was sweeter far than honey,
Was stronger far than wine.
5   They brewed it and they drank it,
And lay in a blessed swound[2]
For days and days together
In their dwellings underground.

II

There rose a king in Scotland,
10   A fell[3] man to his foes,
He smote the Picts in battle,
He hunted them like roes[4].
Over miles of the red mountain
He hunted as they fled,
15   And strewed the dwarfish bodies
Of the dying and the dead.

III

Summer came in the country,
Red was the heather bell;
But the manner of the brewing
20   Was none alive to tell.
In graves that were like children's
On many a mountain head,
The Brewsters of the Heather
Lay numbered with the dead.

IV

25   The king in the red moorland
Rode on a summer's day;
And the bees hummed, and the curlews
Cried beside the way.
The king rode, and was angry,
30   Black was his brow and pale;
To rule in a land of heather
And lack the Heather Ale.

V

It fortuned than his vassals [5],
Riding free on the heath,
35 Came on a stone that was fallen
And vermin hid beneath.
Rudely plucked from their hiding,
Never a word they spoke:
A son and his aged father —
40 Last of the dwarfish folk.

VI

The king sat high on his charger [6]
He looked on the little men;
And the dwarfish and swarthy couple
Looked at the king again.
45 Down by the shore he had them;
And there on the giddy brink —
'I will give you life, ye vermin,
For the secret of the drink.'

VII

There stood the son and father
50 And they looked high and low;
The heather was red around them,
The sea rumbled below.
And up and spoke the father,
Shrill was his voice to hear:
55 'I have a word in private,
A word for the royal ear.

VIII

'Life is dear to the aged,
And honour a little thing;
I would gladly sell the secret,'
60 Quoth [7] the Pict to the king.
His voice was small as a sparrow's,
And shrill and wonderful clear;
'I would gladly sell my secret,
Only my son I fear.

IX

65 'For life is a little matter
And death is nought to the young;
And I dare not sell my honour
Under the eye of my son.
Take *him*, O king, and bind him,
70 And cast him far in the deep;
And it's I will tell the secret
That I have sworn to keep.'

X

They took the son and bound him,
Neck and heels in a thong,
75 And a lad took him and swung him,
And flung him far and strong,
And the sea swallowed his body,
Like that of a child of ten, —
And there on the cliff stood the father,
80 Last of the dwarfish men.

XI

'True was the word I told you:
Only my son I feared;
For I doubt the sapling courage
That goes without the beard.
85 But now in vain is the torture,
Fire shall never avail[8];
Here dies in my bosom
The secret of Heather Ale.'

1 lang-syne: long ago   2 swound: state of unconsciousness
3 fell: cruel   4 roes: small deer
5 vassals: servants   6 charger: war horse
7 quoth: said   8 avail: have power

QUESTIONS

1. Read verses 1 and 2 (lines 1–16).
    'The bonny bells of heather' (line 1).

    What mood is set up by this phrase? How is this mood continued in the
    ideas and word choice in the rest of verse 1 (lines 1–8)? (4)

2. The mood changes suddenly in verse 2.

    What does the mood change to? Show how the ideas and word choice
    contribute to this change of mood. (4)

3. Read verses 3 and 4 (lines 17–32).

    Pick out two references to colours in these lines. Explain how they may
    have a symbolic significance in addition to the basic, literal meaning. (4)

4. 'graves that were like children's' (line 21).

    (a) What does this detail reveal about the physical nature of the Picts?
    (b) How does this phrase affect your response to the fate of the Picts? (2)

5. 'The king sat high on his charger,
    He looked on the little men;
    And the dwarfish and swarthy couple
    Looked at the king again.' (lines 41–44)

    Show how the poet's ideas and word choice suggest the attitude of the
    king to the Picts, and the Picts' attitude to the king. (4)

6. Read verses 7–9 (lines 49–72).

    In your own words, explain the reasons the father gives which convince
    his captors he is willing to betray the secret. Explain also why he asks
    them to murder his son. (3)

7. Read the last verse. (lines 81–88).

    In your own words, explain the true reasons the father gives for having
    had his son killed. (2)

8. Look back at verse 1 and the way the Picts are portrayed. Why does the old Pict's desperate defence of his honour seem surprising after this?   (1)

9. Referring closely to the text, explain how any **two** of the following contribute to the overall effect of the poem:
    (i) the description of the setting, including details of the weather and the landscape
    (ii) the use of direct speech
    (iii) the use of sound in techniques such as alliteration, onomatopoeia, rhyme and rhythm   (6)

Total Marks: 30

PART TWO

WRITING SKILLS

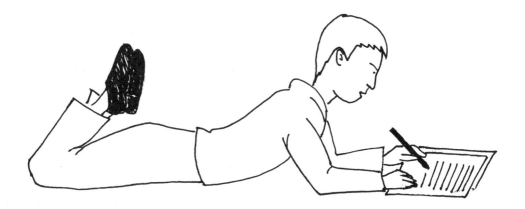

PUNCTUATION (1)

What is a sentence?

A sentence is a group of words which makes sense standing on its own. It contains a **subject** (usually the person doing the action) and a **verb** (the action itself). It doesn't matter how long or short it is; a sentence is a sentence when it is a completed statement.

Stephanie fell asleep.

After spending nearly two hours working out at the gym, Stephanie struggled home, lay down on the sofa to watch television but instantly dozed off.

Each of these statements is a sentence; the second one just goes into rather more detail.

On the other hand, a group of words like

After spending nearly two hours working out at the gym . . .

is *not* a sentence because it is not complete; it leads us to expect something else to follow.

FOR PRACTICE:

(a) In the following passage from John Buchan's *The Thirty-Nine Steps*, the completed sentences have been run into each other with commas rather than being separated by full stops. This is a common error, sometimes called the 'comma splice'.

Rewrite the passage correctly, replacing commas with full stops where appropriate. (Note that some of the commas are correct.)

I had before me a choice of route, I chose a ridge which made an angle with the one I was on, and so would put a deep glen between me and my enemies, the exercise had warmed my blood, I was beginning to enjoy myself amazingly, as I went I breakfasted on the dusty remnants of the ginger biscuits, I knew very little about the country, I hadn't a notion what I was going to do, I trusted to the strength of my legs, but I was well aware that those behind me would be familiar with the lie of the land, and that my ignorance would be a heavy handicap, I saw in front of me a sea of hills, rising very high toward the south, but northwards breaking down into broad ridges which separated wide and shallow dales, that seemed as good a direction to take as any other.

(b) Rewrite this passage from Mary Shelley's *Frankenstein*, again changing commas to full stops or question marks where appropriate.

As I said these words, I perceived in the gloom a figure which stole from behind a clump of trees near me, I stood fixed, gazing intently, I could not be mistaken, a flash of lightning illuminated the object and revealed its shape plainly to me, its gigantic stature and the deformity of its aspect instantly informed me that it was the wretch, the filthy demon, to whom I had given life, what did he there, could he be the murderer of my brother, no sooner did that idea cross my imagination than I became convinced of its truth, my teeth chattered, I was forced to lean against a tree for support, the figure passed me quickly and I lost it in the gloom.

PUNCTUATION (2)

Avoiding repetitive sentences

Once you are sure that your sentences are properly divided up you can move on to develop more complex and stylish sentence structures. Often people use too many short, simple sentences; sometimes, they write in long, rambling ones. The best writers, however, achieve a variety of sentence lengths and use different joining methods to avoid repetition and monotony.

(a) Look at this passage from a pupil's narrative essay:

> It was early in the morning. I made my way towards the house. I saw the front door was open. I hurried to my father's room. I wanted to discover how much he knew. I wanted to know whether he knew anything about what had happened last night. I went into the room. It was clear from his face that he already knew all about it. I wondered what I should say.

There are no comma splices in this extract. Technically, it is written and punctuated correctly but it is not a very effective piece of writing. The sentences are of similar length — mostly very short — and they tend to begin with 'I', giving a monotonous effect.

♦ Try to improve the passage by joining some of the sentences into longer ones. This can be done by avoiding some of the repetition of 'I', and by using a variety of joining methods such as conjunctions.(Look ahead to *Punctuation (4)* for some further advice on this.)

(b) This paragraph from another pupil's essay on Scottish poetry uses repetitive sentence structure. The points could also be put in better order. Rewrite it, avoiding some of the repetition and putting similar points beside each other or in the same sentence.

> A poem that I liked was 'Listen tae the Teacher' by Nancy Nicolson. In this poem the Scots language gives a rhythm which makes the poem like a song. This poem is about a small boy being confused whether to speak in Scots or English. The poem has a chorus which is entertaining. The poem sounds more effective when it is set to music. 'Listen tae the Teacher' uses both Scots language and standard English.

PUNCTUATION (3)

Long and short sentences

So far we have looked at ways of avoiding too many short sentences. But there are occasions when short sentences can sometimes be used very effectively to create a contrast with longer ones.

(a) This passage comes from a short story called *The Kite* by W. Somerset Maugham.

> Their ambition was to have a bigger kite than anyone else and a kite that would go higher. They had long given up a cord, for the kite they gave Herbert on his birthday was seven feet high, and they used piano wire wound round a drum. But that did not satisfy Herbert. Somehow or other he had heard of a box-kite which had been invented by somebody, and the idea appealed to him at once.

This extract consists of four sentences, with the reader's attention being drawn to the third one because it is shorter than the ones on either side of it. The point that stands out from the paragraph is that Herbert was not satisfied. The third sentence could easily be joined on to the second one (as 'but' is generally used as a joining word) but this would spoil the effect of contrast.

(b) In this extract from a short story called *The Bike* by Fred Urquhart, the author is describing a girl called Annie who saved very hard to afford a new bike.

> But the three years were long when she saw the number of pies the other girls consumed and the bottles of lemonade they tilted to their dry mouths. Sometimes she thought it wasn't worth it; the bike seemed as far away as ever. And she would look at the little penny-bank-book that was all that she had to show for her scrimping, and she thought often of blowing the whole amount on a new coat or on a trip to Blackpool. But she sternly set her mind against the temptations that the other girls whispered to her. And at last she got her bike.

Here the short last sentence works as a climax to the paragraph. After all the years of saving and sacrificing, Annie has at last achieved her ambition.

One of the rules of good writing is:

Vary the pace of your essay by using different sentence lengths.

(c) On the following page is an extract from an essay written by a pupil who was in a hurry to finish his homework. He has poured out all his ideas one after the other without varying the sentence structures.

♦ Read it over and make a list of some of the faults of style and punctuation. You will see that there are several punctuation errors here, particularly comma splices.

♦ Try rewriting the passage so that both long and short sentences are used. One or two well-placed short sentences will make all the difference.

♦ The extract is also rather long for a single paragraph; think of a place where a new paragraph should start.

♦ You can make any other alterations to the wording or expression that you feel would be an improvement, such as removing some of the repetition. However, the aim of the exercise is basically to improve the standard of the way this passage is written rather than to change it into something else altogether.

I ran through the darkened streets, in and out of alleyways with my coat flying behind me. I heard the shouting of the men as their dogs searched the surrounding area, I stopped and listened more closely and then moved on. The escape had turned out to be harder than I thought it would be at first and with two of the other escapees caught there was not much chance of me surviving the night. I had been jailed five years before for committing a crime, I had not even been involved in the crime, it had all been my so called friend Robbie's fault, he had been the one who told them everything. What he hadn't told them was that he was the one who had done it and it wasn't me. Finally I reached the field where we had arranged to meet if anything went wrong, no-one was there. I climbed a tree and waited a while but no-one came along and I could hear the police dogs barking in the distance.

PUNCTUATION (4)

Methods of joining sentences

Some short sentences can be merged into longer ones simply by avoiding repetition but there are numerous words which help to improve the flow of sentences. The grammatical names for these are **conjunctions** and **relative pronouns** but it is perhaps more important to know how to use these than to know the technical names for them.

Even the youngest writer uses simple conjunctions like 'and' and 'but'. At this level, however, you should try to use a greater variety of conjunctions such as:

BECAUSE	ALTHOUGH	SINCE	IF	UNLESS
UNTIL	WHILE	AS	WHEN	THOUGH
	BEFORE	AFTER		

Sentences can be joined by placing the conjunction in between the two sentences —

> *We waited for hours. We were determined to secure a seat.*
> *We waited for hours **because** we were determined to secure a seat.*

— or at the start of the first sentence:

> *We waited for hours. We didn't manage to secure a seat.*
> ***Although** we waited for hours, we didn't manage to secure a seat.*

A relative pronoun, such as **who** (for a person) or **which** (for a thing) refers back to a noun already used in the sentence and links it to the next statement.

For instance, these two sentences —

> *The Italian player was bought for £3,000,000. He has gone down well with the fans.*

— could be joined with the relative pronoun **who**:

> *The Italian player **who** was bought for £3,000,000 has gone down well with the fans.*

Note that the relative pronoun usually goes beside the noun that it relates to:

> *By the time we arrived home the programme **which** we wanted to see had nearly finished.*

The following passage is adapted from the story *The Canterville Ghost* by Oscar Wilde but the punctuation has been changed. Rewrite the passage using conjunctions and relative pronouns to join some of the sentences. There are fifteen sentences in this paragraph; using the joining methods suggested above, try to reduce the paragraph to about six or seven sentences.

It was four days after these curious incidents. A funeral started from Canterville Chase. The hearse was drawn by a black horse. It carried on its head a great tuft of ostrich-plumes. The leaden coffin was covered by a rich purple pall. On it was embroidered in gold the Canterville coat-of-arms. By the side of the hearse and the coaches walked the servants. They carried lighted torches. These made the whole procession wonderfully impressive. Lord Canterville had come up specially from Wales. He was the chief mourner. He sat in the first carriage along with little Virginia. In the last carriage came Mrs Umney. She had been frightened by the ghost for more than fifty years of her life. She had a right to see the last of him.

PUNCTUATION (5)

Starting sentences with linking words

Conjunctions and relative pronouns join sentences together, but there are other words which can be used at the start of a sentence to help connect one idea to the next, without actually joining the sentences. These words are particularly useful in factual and argumentative writing or in critical essays on literature.

Adding on similar points	*Making points different from the previous one*	*Drawing a conclusion*
furthermore	however	thus
in the same way	on the other hand	therefore
similarly	in contrast	hence
moreover	nevertheless	consequently
in addition to		

Remember that these words begin a new sentence but should not be used to join two sentences into one. Take particular care with 'however', which is often misused as a conjunction.

I wasn't looking forward to the party, however I knew I'd end up going along anyway.

'However' cannot be used in this way as it creates a 'comma splice'. Either:

(i) Use two sentences:

I wasn't looking forward to the party. However, I knew I'd end up going along anyway.

or

(ii) Replace 'however' with the conjunction 'but':

I wasn't looking forward to the party but I knew I'd end up going along anyway.

Rewrite the following paragraph, using linking words from the list on the previous page at the beginning of some of the sentences to improve the flow of ideas at the points marked *.

There is no doubt that the internet is revolutionising the way we do business. The existence of email makes communication much quicker. * Businesses can make contact with many more potential customers than before. It is now possible to order almost any goods, from books to groceries, over the internet. * This does not suit everyone. Some potential customers find unwanted emails as annoying as the junk mail that comes through their letter boxes. * Many people prefer to see what they are buying first. * Internet shopping is something that everyone will have to get used to as it is certain to grow in the next few years.

PUNCTUATION (6)

Colons and semi-colons

If you are confident about the use of full stops and commas, you can try to be a little more adventurous and make use of colons and semi-colons.

A colon (:) is used to introduce a list, an example or a fuller explanation of the previous statement:

> *There was only one possible explanation: the car had been stolen.*

A semi-colon (;) can be used
> to separate two sentences which are in some way closely related;
> to create a contrast or balance between two statements;
> to separate a list of phrases.

Look at these examples from Charlotte Bronte's novel *Jane Eyre*:

(i)   I, supposing he had done with me, prepared to return to the house; again, however, I heard him call 'Jane'!

(ii)   The stillness of the early morning slumbered everywhere; the curtains were yet drawn over the servants' chamber windows; little birds were just twittering in the blossom-blanched orchard-trees, whose boughs drooped like white garlands over the wall enclosing one side of the yard; the carriage horses stamped from time to time in their closed stables: all else was still.

Discuss why semi-colons have been used here. Could full stops have been used instead? Or commas?

This description of the Palace of Versailles was adapted from a passage in a travel book called *The Innocents Abroad* by the American writer Mark Twain. Rewrite the passage, inserting either a colon or semi-colon wherever you see a *.

> There is one reason above all others why Versailles is worth a pilgrimage to see* everything is on so gigantic a scale. Nothing is small* nothing is cheap. The statues are all large* the palace is grand* the park covers a fair-sized country* the avenues are interminable. Some people have been very critical of Louis XIV* he is accused of spending two hundred millions of dollars in creating this marvellous park, when bread was so scarce with some of his subjects* but I have forgiven him now.

WORD CHOICE

(1) Avoiding overused words

Poor writers resort to the same simple words over and over again. Among the favourites are *get*, *a lot*, *so*, *thing* and *nice*. There's nothing *wrong* with these words: we use them all the time in conversation, but in writing there is usually a more exact or interesting word that could be used.

Get, for instance, can have all kinds of meanings:

> *She got a newspaper on her way to work.*
> *He got to the bus stop just as the bus was leaving.*
> *Make sure you don't get lost!*
> *He's getting old.*
> *He got an unexpected letter through the post.*

♦ Can you think of other ways of wording these sentences without using 'get'?

♦ In the passage which follows the writer has overused the word 'get'. Rewrite it using more varied word choice. In some cases, there will be an alternative verb to use; in others, the word 'get' can simply be missed out altogether.

> I got in through a side door which was hanging from its hinges. It made a long eerie creak as I pushed it open. I heard the sound of breaking glass and laughing. As I got closer the passage got narrower. Eventually I had to crawl. When I got out in the open I got onto the balcony of the warehouse. I could see that the two groups of men in the courtyard below were getting ready to exchange briefcases. There were handshakes all round. Everything seemed to be taking so long that I wished I'd got some food at the shop at the corner of the street before coming in, for it seemed like I was going to be stuck there all night. It was then that I realised what was going to happen: from my high-up vantage point I could see one of the men slowly getting a gun out of his jacket pocket.

♦ One dictionary gives the following definitions for the word 'get':

achieve	*acquire*	*attain*	*earn*
fetch	*obtain*	*purchase*	*grab*
seize	*arrange*	*catch*	*receive*

Rewrite the following sentences, replacing 'get' with one of the above. (Some minor changes to the wording of the sentence may be necessary).

(i) We just managed to get the train minutes before it left.

(ii) I managed to get a glazier to come and fix the window.

(iii) By changing jobs she ended up getting a much higher salary.

(iv) I'll have to get another tin of paint to finish off the decorating.

(v) The policeman got hold of the thief who was trying to escape through the back window.

♦ 'Get' is also used with many different prepositions — that is, small words that show the position of one thing in relation to another (such as *at*, *to*, *over*, and so on).

Find a word from column B which corresponds with the words in column A.

A	B
Get back	annoy
Get across (information)	return
Get at	convey
Get over (e.g., a difficulty or an illness)	disembark
Get by	surmount
Get round	prepare
Get out of	evade
Get off	escape
Get ready	survive

A lot is an informal, conversational expression which is best avoided in writing. Instead of saying *a lot* or *lots of*, use other terms which relate to quantity or number such as *many*, *much*, *most*, *a number of*, *a great deal of*, *numerous*, and so on. There are lots of alternatives to *a lot*!

♦ Rewrite the following sentences, replacing 'a lot' or 'lots' with a more formal and exact term.

(i) On the first morning at my new school I met lots of people I had never seen before.

(ii) I had a lot of difficulty trying to work out the answers to the Maths questions.

(iii) He gave me a lot of different explanations for what he had done, but it was clear that these were just excuses.

So is a 'lazy' choice as a joining word: with a little thought it is always possible to come up with another word to use.

For example, instead of joining two sentences by putting *so* between them, you can put a conjunction like *as* in front of the first one. In written English

As Craig was seventeen, he started having driving lessons.

is better style than

Craig was seventeen so he started having driving lessons.

Where the second sentence explains the reason for what was said in the first sentence, the expression 'so that' is better than 'so':

*The detective hid behind the trees **so that** he could see if anyone was approaching the house.*

♦ Rewrite the following sentences, using more original joining methods than 'so':

(i) Our car had been in an accident so the garage provided us with a courtesy car.

(ii) He left the house at 7a.m. so he could be there in plenty of time.

(iii) Extra funds are needed if the club is to continue so we are going to hold a jumble sale.

Thing is a vague word that has no specific meaning — it applies to whatever is being talked about. Again, in writing you should use a more specific word. For instance, when writing an essay, don't say:

One thing about this poem which appealed to me was . . .

It would be better to write

One aspect / feature of the poem which appealed to me was . . .

Nice is another overworked word which is used in conversation to describe anything pleasant, whether it is a person, food, a tune, a film or anything else. In writing, a wider range of descriptive words (adjectives) should be employed to explain why the subject is 'nice'.

♦ Make a list of describing words which could be used as substitutes for 'nice' in each of these cases:

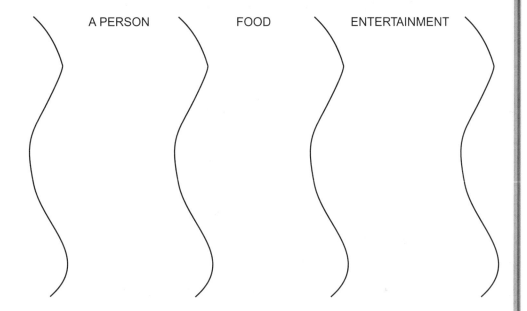

A PERSON   FOOD   ENTERTAINMENT

(2) Expanding your range of vocabulary

Many students feel that they know what they want to say, but can't put it into words. Some can explain their point of view clearly when talking but find it much harder to do this in writing.

The best way to increase your range of vocabulary is by reading widely — not only by reading class or home readers but by reading good quality journalism.

Each day newspapers like *The Guardian*, *The Scotsman* or *The Times* contain short pieces giving the paper's view on topical subjects. These items are called editorials and can usually be found near the centre of the paper. An editorial is similar to a piece of argumentative or discursive writing, in which the 'for' and 'against' views are explained. Reading these regularly will help improve your style of writing.

Another tactic, which calls for a more organised and systematic approach, is to keep a list of new words that you meet in the course of your reading. You should then look these up in the dictionary and copy out the meaning.

♦ The words below can all be used to describe people — their characteristics, moods, attitudes and personalities.

(a) The words and their meanings have been mixed up. Copy out the words and write out the correct meaning beside each, using your dictionary to help if necessary.

(Group 1)

	Word		Meaning
1	Audacious	A	sociable, fond of being with people
2	Benevolent	B	full of enthusiasm, energy and ideas
3	Culpable	C	behaving in different ways at different times; unpredictable
4	Callous	D	shy and embarrassed, especially in public
5	Gregarious	E	not reliable or trustworthy
6	Irresponsible	F	deserving to be blamed
7	Inhibited	G	kind and helpful
8	Inconsistent	H	heartless, cruel, unfeeling
9	Dynamic	I	strong, worthy, reliable (e.g., in support of something)
10	Stalwart	J	very daring

(Group 2)

	Word		Meaning
1	Illustrious	A	showing an excess of enthusiasm for something
2	Prejudiced	B	famous and respected
3	Penitent	C	liable to sudden, unexpected outbursts
4	Rational	D	generous and forgiving
5	Inhospitable	E	not welcoming
6	Magnanimous	F	having formed unfair opinions in advance
7	Volatile	G	easily made angry
8	Fanatical	H	reasonable; able to think things through
9	Notorious	I	deeply sorry for having done wrong
10	Irritable	J	well-known for something bad

(b) Rewrite the following sentences, using suitable words from these lists to fill the gaps:

(i) Although he was usually a very friendly person, he behaved towards the visitors in a rather _____ way.

(ii) The behaviour of the _____ criminal had clearly been _____ but when the crime was discovered he showed a very _____ attitude.

(iii) The Member of Parliament was asked several times to explain his Party's views on the issue, but his answers were _____.

(iv) At school he seemed very _____ , rarely mixing with people or taking part in anything, but once he started working he developed into a much more _____ person.

(v) Brian's enthusiasm for the team was so great that it was bordering on the _____.

(vi) The vet was shocked when he heard of the man's _____ treatment of the dog.

(vii) When questioned the boy could offer no _____ explanation of why he had broken the window.

♦ The words below can all be used in connection with public life — government, employment, business, administration and so on.

(a) The words and their meanings have been mixed up. Copy out the words and write out the correct meaning beside each, using your dictionary to help if necessary.

	Word		*Meaning*
1	bureaucracy	A	a set of rules governing an organisation
2	centralisation	B	process of choosing people by voting
3	personnel	C	person lower in rank or importance
4	systematic	D	system of officials and departments involved in running a country or organisation
5	hierarchy	E	working according to a planned and well-ordered approach
6	productivity	F	arrangement of people in order of importance
7	subsidiary	G	rate of production, in industry for example
8	subordinate	H	bringing everything under central control (e.g., of a head office)
9	election	I	a company or business of secondary importance, owned by a larger organisation
10	constitution	J	the people employed within an organisation, company, etc.

(b) Try writing sentences of your own using some of the above words.

(3) Words that people often confuse

Some words sound very similar but are spelt differently. The following often cause difficulties.

allowed
having permission to do something

aloud
loud enough to be heard

breath (noun)
air drawn into and sent out of the lungs

breathe (verb)
the action of breathing

cloths
pieces of fabric

clothes
items worn on the body; garments

councillor
a member of a local government body

counsellor
someone who gives advice and guidance (adviser)

eligible
suitable to be chosen
(e.g., for a husband)

illegible
writing that is hard to read

hear
to be able to listen to a sound

here
place (opposite of there)

moral
relating to choices between right
and wrong

morale
level of confidence

practice (noun)
as in: music practice, a
doctor's practice, etc.

practise (verb)
as in: I practise playing
the piano every day

right
opposite of wrong

write
to produce letters
on a surface with
a pen, etc.

stationary
not moving

stationery
paper, envelopes and
other writing materials

N.B. station**e** ry
     n
     v
     e
     l
     o
     p
     e

Copy out these sentences, filling each gap with a suitable word from the list above:

(i)   Once she reaches the age of seventy, my gran will be _____
       for a free television licence.

(ii)   The house was so quiet that I could almost _____ myself _____ .

(iii) My neighbour was so fed up with the state of the road that he decided to _____ a letter of complaint to the local _____ .

(iv) The _____ of the story seemed to be that in the end people get what they deserve.

(v) As a child Kevin had always been _____ to do anything he wanted.

(vi) 'I can't read a word of this,' complained the teacher. 'You _____ in a completely _____ way.'

(vii) After years of having to work increasingly long hours the _____ of the workforce was very low.

(viii) Anyone who wants to be a professional musician has to _____ for several hours every day.

(ix) Accidents can occur when a pedestrian suddenly steps out from behind a _____ vehicle.

(x) It was a good idea in theory, but it was difficult to put into _____ .

Do you often mix up THERE, THEIR and THEY'RE?

REMINDER

there — refers to place, as in 'over there'.

there's — short for 'there is'.

their — belonging to them, as in 'their house'.

they're — short for 'they are'.

♦ Copy out these sentences, filling each gap with a suitable word from the list on the previous page:

(i) _____ no point in asking if you can borrow _____ mobile phone; they'll never let you have it.

(ii) If _____ train's running to time, _____ due to arrive about 7 pm.

(iii) _____ only one route into the village: a long winding path up the hillside.

(iv) 'O Christmas Tree, O Christmas Tree, your branches green delight us.
_____ green when summer days are bright;
_____ green when winter snow is white.'

Other words are confused because of the use of apostrophes.

REMINDER
Apostrophes are generally used for two purposes:
Where letters are missed out as in **don't** which is short for **do not**.
To show ownership as in **the girl's shoes**. If the word girl was in the plural (i.e., more than one girl) then the apostrophe would go after the letter 's': **the girls' shoes**.

Take care with the following pairs of words:

its
of it / belonging to it
e.g., The car was in its garage.

it's
short for it is
e.g., It's an old story.

whose
belonging to
e.g., Whose are these clothes?

who's
short for who is
e.g., Who's coming to the party?

your
belonging to you
e.g., Don't forget your scarf.

you're
short for you are
e.g., You're not being serious.

◆ Copy out these sentences, filling each gap with a suitable word from the list on the previous page:

(i) _____ nearly time for Santa to come. (*it's* or *its*?)

(ii) _____ is the present with the red bow on it? (*whose* or *who's*?)

(iii) The weather forecast says _____ going to be a white Christmas. (*it's* or *its*?)

(iv) _____ going to help put up the Christmas decorations? (*who's* or *whose*?)

(v) Are you going to hang up _____ stocking on Christmas Eve? (*your* or *you're*?)

(vi) Every year the store puts up a giant Christmas tree in _____ toy department. (*it's* or *its*?)

Advice on Essay Writing Technique

Essays can take many different forms:

Creative and imaginative writing
♦ a short story
♦ an account of a personal experience

Factual writing
♦ a report
♦ A discussion of views for and against an issue

Obviously, different approaches are needed for each kind of essay, but some guidelines apply to them all:

(a)   General guidelines

Make a plan

Note down your thoughts in any order. Then try to put them into a better sequence. In general, you should have some idea of how the essay is to end before you actually start writing it. This will save you running out of material half way through and having to start again with another topic.

Divide your essay into paragraphs

Begin a new paragraph whenever you move on to a different aspect of the topic.

Vary your sentence lengths

Re-read your essay and check to see whether you have used any of the suggestions on pages 68–75.

Do a rough copy

Then re-read it all at one go, as the reader will do. Check that you have not repeated yourself, or used similar words too often or too close to each other. Check spelling and punctuation. Then, when you are satisfied with your work, rewrite it or retype it.

(b) Creative and Imaginative Writing

These guidelines apply particularly to writing stories and accounts of personal experiences.

Concentrate on characters rather than events

Don't try to make your story full of action: it is much better to have a small, manageable number of characters and to explain *why* they act as they do: what are they thinking or feeling while the action is developing?

There should also be some development in your characters. The main one should change in some way as a result of the experiences he / she undergoes in the course of the story. Such developments might be along the lines of:

* growth towards maturity;
* learning the lessons of your mistakes;
* becoming less prejudiced, etc.

Use some direct speech

Real people talk to each other. In your essay you might therefore introduce some conversation to bring the characters to life. Don't overdo this, however; otherwise your story will read more like a drama script.

Remember to punctuate your direct speech properly, putting inverted commas round the actual words spoken:

> *"Get a move on," shouted Mike. "We're going to be late!"*

Include some description

This needn't be obvious description (what a person looks like and so on). It is more effective to use description to create an atmosphere. If you can include the occasional comparison using imagery (such as a simile or metaphor), this will add greatly to the effect of your writing.

Aim for an opening that will attract the reader's attention

It's easier said than done, of course, but your introduction should in some way raise the readers' expectations by saying something that makes them want to read on. You might, for example, start by referring to what happens at the end of the story, with the rest of the essay recapping on the sequence of events that led up to that ending.

♦ Look at the following examples of opening paragraphs from pupils' writing. Discuss what they lead you to expect in the rest of the story.

Mum used to think we were mad, spending all our spare time playing near the canal. She always used to say, 'Be careful, Gail!' Of course, I never listened to her and just thought she was being over-protective.

'You can do it, Alan!' All his friends were urging him on. It was just a harmless dare: once he'd jumped off the bridge he could easily swim to the bank.

'Come on, Alan. What are you waiting for?'

Silence. It was essential. The nightly patrol went past and my heart seemed to stop beating. It had to be tonight. Months of preparation all led up to this moment. There would never be a better opportunity.

Home sweet home. Home is where the heart is. I have a home. A comfortable house, with large rooms and a spacious garden. And yet here I am, sitting on a park bench getting soaked to the skin.

WRITING ASSIGNMENTS

The following incidents were recently reported in the newspapers. Choose one of these reports and use it as the basis for a story of your own. You could, for example, imagine that you are one of the people involved. What were your thoughts and feelings during the event? Try to imagine what the people were like. What was going through their minds? What were their reasons for doing what they did? Use some direct speech to make your characters more lifelike.

Wayward son takes judge's clothes

JUDGE John Wroath, 63, from Cowes, Isle of Wight, was due to hear a case when he discovered his son John, 30, a singer and bass guitarist with the appropriately named rock band The Wayward Sons, was performing a gig in his wig and robes.

Fortunately, the Portsmouth County Court sitting was cancelled, but the judge has made it clear the attire is out of bounds. "If I ever find him near them again, John will feel the full force of my law. One has to respect the dignity and responsibility of my office."

His son intends to perform in robes and wig again — from a fancy dress shop.

Dark secret

A woman who as a schoolgirl 25 years ago smashed the glass in two lamp posts at Purley, Surrey, has sent the council £20 as "a token of my sorrow and guilt". She wrote from Germany: "This moment of wildness has never left my memory."

Weeded out

A keen gardener, Kaye Holland, 65, unearthed the gold wedding ring that his wife Irene, 63, lost when she threw it at him during an argument 25 years ago at their home in Tiverton, Devon.

Boys keep loot

Three schoolboys who found buried treasure will be allowed to keep it after efforts to trace the owners failed. David Jones, 16, Daniel Eccles, 13, and his 11-year-old brother Damien found silverware and jewellery in a hole on a canal bank near Halsall, Lancashire. Police believe it was hidden by a burglar.

Driver in wrong lane of A1 survives

A driver escaped with cuts and bruises yesterday after driving the wrong way on a motorway overtaking lane and colliding head-on with a lorry. The woman, 29, was returning home to Washington, Tyne and Wear, after an argument with a friend. She missed her turning on the A1(M) and made a U-turn.

Rail escape

A man aged 31 walked away unhurt after lying on the track at Bournemouth station beneath an express train.

Fear of flying

A plane carrying 400 holiday-makers bound for Minorca was delayed at Manchester Airport for more than two hours after a frightened passenger demanded to get off. The family's luggage had to be removed from the hold.

First woman trainer

The British Boxing Board of Control has granted a boxing trainer's licence to a woman for the first time. Babs Spear, 41, from Brunton, Devon, who is 5ft 2in, trains Richie Wenton, 27, a super bantamweight champion. She said: "I know I will be up against some animosity because I am a woman in a man's game."

(c) **Factual and argumentative writing**

This kind of essay will be written in a different style from a story or a personal essay. It will tend to be more **formal** (see page 14). It will explain your personal views on the subject and may therefore use the first person ('I') but it will not be written in a 'chatty' or light-hearted style.

A typical question of this kind might be

BOXING:
SHOULD IT BE BANNED?

Here is a recommended method of planning and writing an essay on this topic.

1. *Do some research*

   Look up encyclopaedias, newspapers, magazines, the internet or any similar source of information.

2. *Make a list of the points you want to include*

   You might do this under the headings 'for' and 'against'. Try to list your points in ascending order of importance — that is, from minor points to major points, keeping the most convincing arguments to the last.

3. *Draw up a paragraph plan*

   Paragraph 1: outline the subject under discussion, showing why it is a controversial one. State your own view which will be developed in the rest of the essay.

   Paragraphs 2 / 3: discuss the opposite view from your own.

Paragraphs 4 / 5:   outline the reasons for your own view, backed up with actual examples from your research.

Paragraph 6:   balance the two sides and reach a clear conclusion.

Begin each paragraph with a TOPIC SENTENCE, i.e., a sentence which introduces the general idea which the rest of the paragraph develops in detail.

(d)   *An example*

Here are two extracts from a pupil's essay on the subject of Boxing. This is the introductory paragraph:

> *There is no doubt that boxing is a very controversial sport and there are many points of view on whether it should be banned or not. These views come mainly from people in the medical profession and, of course, the fans of the sport. I find myself in the ironic situation of believing that it should be banned, and yet I enjoy watching it whenever I have the opportunity.*

Marker's opinion: The opening sentence is clear enough, though not especially original. The last sentence, however, is rather good as it shows the writer is aware that this is not a simple, clear-cut issue.

In a later paragraph, the writer moves on to consider some of the drawbacks of boxing:

> *The sport has witnessed many unsavoury incidents throughout the last few years. The best-known cases are those of Mohammed Ali who developed boxing-related Parkinson's Disease and Michael Watson who nearly died in the ring while fighting Chris Eubank in 1991. It is events such as these which have prompted the British Medical Association to campaign against the sport. One medical expert made the point in simple, graphic terms when he said that 'blows to the head cause the brain to move in the skull like a jelly in a bowl.'*

Marker's opinion: The opening sentence of this paragraph is a successful topic sentence. [What does it do?] The sentences that follow make good use of research evidence.

♦ Discuss (either in pairs, groups or as a whole class) what might be said in favour of boxing. Make a list of these points and grade them in order from the least important to the most convincing. Then write a paragraph continuing the above essay, using this topic sentence as the opening:

> **Although many people see boxing as amounting to nothing more than violence, those who take part in the sport see matters very differently . . .**

Useful phrases:

These can be used at the start of sentences to help your paragraphs flow. They are useful not just for the essay on Boxing, but for any essay of this type.

It is certainly true that . . .
In the same way . . .
More importantly . . .
Of greater significance is the fact that . . .
Perhaps one of the most convincing arguments is . . .
Nevertheless, a number of criticisms of this view come to mind . . .
A more serious objection is . . .
The opponents of . . . may argue that . . .
While it is true that . . .
The evidence would therefore suggest that . . .

WRITING ASSIGNMENT

Something should be done about it!

It shouldn't be allowed!

Think of an issue that YOU feel strongly about and on which people hold various opinions.

Write an essay on the topic using the guidelines given above. Remember to take a restrained, balanced approach without using too much emotive language (see page 13) — even if it is a subject that you have very strong views about.

100 words that people find hard to spell

(a) Words containing double letters

accept	committee	interruption	rearrange
accident	disappear	necessary	recommend
admission	disapproval	occasionally	sufficient
appealing	dissatisfied	opportunity	surroundings
appropriate	exaggerate	opposition	tomorrow
arrangement	excess	predecessor	travelled
basically	hurriedly	possession	
beginning	immediately	professional	

(b) Difficulties with vowels (especially 'a' or 'e')

character	imaginary	privilege	sentence
definite	independent	relevant	separate
definitely	intelligent	resemblance	statement
emphasise	medicine	responsible	tendency
existence	primitive	sensible	

(c) Words containing 'ie' or 'ei'

achievement	foreign	receive	yield
belief	height	reign	
believe	neighbour	seize	
fierce	quiet	shield	

(d) Words containing 'ou'

conscious	humour	routine	thorough
favourite	humorous	thought	through

(e) Other difficulties

advertisement	century	literature	rhythm
already	college	maintain	satisfaction
amateur	development	maintenance	sincerely
argument	excitement	objection	sufficient
authority	fortunate	parallel	usually
beautiful	government	plentiful	writing
business	guarantee	queue	
campaign	knowledge	rhyme	

ACKNOWLEDGEMENTS

We hereby acknowledge the use of copyright material in this book
and are grateful to those for granting this permission.

James Cameron's *TITANIC*
Extract from the Foreword by James Cameron
Reprinted by permission of the publisher Macmillan Publishers London.

TV MOVIE OF THE WEEK
by Barbara Ellen
© Barbara Ellen / The Times 21st December 2000.

DEAD SOULS
by Ian Rankin
Reprinted by permission of the publisher Phoenix.

THE CAT CAME BACK
by Dominic Ryan
Extract from *The Herald* © SMG Newspapers Limited.
Reproduced with permission.

A SUDDEN, SERIOUS BRUSH WITH MORTALITY
by Sandy Strang
Extract from *The Herald* and reprinted by permission of Alexander Strang.

HARRY POTTER AND THE CHAMBER OF SECRETS
by J.K. Rowling
Extract from the Bloomsbury edition © J.K. Rowling 1998 and
reprinted by permission of Christopher Little, Literary Agency.

NORTHERN LIGHTS
by Philip Pullman
Extract from the 1998 edition.
Reprinted by permission of the publisher Scholastic Ltd.

Extract from *MAN AND BOY*
by Tony Parsons
Reprinted by permission of the publisher Harper Collins Publishers Ltd.

Extract from *I KNOW THIS MUCH IS TRUE*
by Wally Lamb
Reprinted by permission of the publisher Harper Collins Publishers Ltd.

CARGOES
from *Selected Poems*
by John Masefield
Reprinted by permission of the The Society of Authors as the
Literary Representative of the Estate of John Masefield.

HAMNAVOE MARKET
by George Mackay-Brown
from his *Selected Poems 1954–1983*
Reprinted by permission of the publisher John Murray (Publishers) Ltd.

ACKNOWLEDGEMENTS (cont'd)

OUT OUT
by Robert Frost from *The Poetry of Robert Frost*
edited by Edward Connery Lathem, the Estate of Robert Frost
and Johnathan Cape as publisher.
Used by permission of The Random House Group Limited.

POEM FOR MY SISTER
from *Dreaming Frankenstein and Collected Poems 1984*
by Liz Lochhead.
Reprinted by permission of the publisher Polygon Press.

The authors would like to record their thanks to Mrs. Rachel Elstone
for her comments at the manuscript stage of this book.

PART ONE: READING SKILLS

TITANIC (1): THE MOVIE QUESTIONS (Page 18)

1. (a) Two of: 'juxtaposition of rich and poor'; 'gender roles played out unto death'; 'the stoicism and nobility of a bygone age'. *(2 marks)*

   (b) Possibilities include:
   'juxtaposition of rich and poor': people of very different backgrounds and levels of wealth were living side by side during the voyage.
   'gender roles played out unto death': men and women at the time were expected to behave in certain clearly defined ways and these standards were maintained even when people were facing death.
   'the stoicism and nobility of a bygone age': bravery and honourable behaviour in a previous period of history. *(1 mark)*

2. Reference to lines 5–6: no one can predict what might happen in life; the worst possible outcome could in fact occur. *(1 mark)*

3. Line 12: 'to bring the event to life' or 'to humanise it'. *(1 mark)*

4. Line 16: 'What to say that hasn't been said?' *(1 mark)*

5. 1,500 is simply a statistic; it is very difficult to imagine the amount of individual human suffering involved. *(2 marks)*

6. The creation of two main characters that the audience can become involved with. *(2 marks)*

7. (a) Line 23: 'an emotional lightning rod'. *(1 mark)*

   (b) The purpose of a lightning rod is to absorb/divert the power of the lightning; in the same way, the audience's emotions about the *Titanic* disaster can be centred round the characters of Jack and Rose. *(1 mark)*

Total: 12 marks

TITANIC (2): THE REVIEW QUESTIONS (Page 20)

1. In the course of making the film, many delays and problems were encountered and these received widespread coverage in the press. The ship did not float or sink as required; the sea was not convincingly stormy; the actors were not believable. *(3 marks)*

2. Paraphrase of 'pretty people in peril': a movie about good-looking people in a dramatic and dangerous situation was always likely to succeed. *(2 marks)*

3. Reference to lines 26–28: in the reviewer's opinion, the two main actors are not well suited. *(2 marks)*

4. (a) Any suitable reference e.g. Lines 23–25: 'American socialite Rose being pursued by DiCaprio's poor, charming artist under the nose of her caddish millionaire fiancé (Billy Zane in cartoon villain mode)'. *(1 mark)*

   (b) Lines 5–6: 'presumably Winslet's voice was more masculine than DiCaprio's'; line 28: 'about as compatible as Laurel and Hardy'. *(1 mark)*

   (c) 'It's perfect family viewing for Christmas Day.' (Lines 34–35). *(1 mark)*

Total: 10 marks

DETECTIVES (1): SHERLOCK HOLMES QUESTIONS (Pages 23–24)

1. Holmes has probably said that they need to learn some more facts ('data') about the case.   *(2 marks)*

2. He wanted to examine the approach to the house carefully in case there were any clues to be discovered. (There are likely to be other acceptable possibilities – e.g., he wanted to be able to arrive at the house discreetly.)   *(2 marks)*

3. The house looked as if it was likely that something unpleasant or evil may have happened there. *(2 marks)*

4. (a) Simile.   *(1 mark)*

   (b) A cataract makes it difficult for light to enter the eye; in the same way, the 'To Let' notice prevented anyone from seeing through the window.   *(2 marks)*

5. Any three suitable inferences e.g.
   - 'a scattered eruption of sickly plants': unhealthy-looking plants had sprung up here and there
   - 'narrow pathway . . . clay and gravel': the pathway was not very wide and was in poor condition
   - 'the whole place was very sloppy from the rain': ground was dirty/untidy/water-logged.   *(3 marks)*

6. Line 16: 'in the vain hope'.   *(1 mark)*

7. (a) Paraphrase of lines 18–19: 'hurried into the house and plunged into a study of the mystery'; e.g. rushed indoors and immediately attempted to solve the case.   *(2 marks)*

   (b) Paraphrase of lines 20–21 e.g. he casually walked up and down the side of the road and stared down as if his mind was elsewhere.   *(2 marks)*

8. The speed at which he was able to notice things.   *(2 marks)*

9. (a) Lines 32–33: 'I had no doubt that he could see a great deal which was hidden from me'.   *(1 mark)*

   (b) Lines 30–31: 'I was unable to see how my companion could hope to learn anything from it'.   *(1 mark)*

10. Gregson had not sealed off the pathway; as a result, many people had walked over it, perhaps destroying vital clues.   *(2 marks)*

11. Irony/sarcasm.   *(2 marks)*

Total: 25 marks

DETECTIVES (2): INSPECTOR REBUS QUESTIONS (Pages 26–27)

1. 'Should have been heading back for the station' and 'something had made him take this detour.' *(2 marks)*

2. (a) The extensive, all-round view.   *(1 mark)*

   (b) His ears were sore for a long time afterwards.   *(1 mark)*

3. Both explanations identified:
   - Suicide: he had deliberately jumped off the cliff.
   - Accident: he had been walking in the dark and a sudden blast of wind had blown him over the edge, or he had tripped and fallen.   *(2 marks)*

4. Three objections identified:
   - It was odd that he had been walking in the middle of the night.
   - It was odd that he was at Salisbury Crags, which was not near his home.
   - It had been a wet night but he did not use his car to get there.   *(3 marks)*

5. Recognition of the ironic juxtaposition of something serious and historic beside a place of entertainment.
(*2 marks*)

6. Any four of the following:

   - Roughcast covering of the walls was stained
   - Leaking plumbing
   - Broken paving slabs
   - Wood in the window frames was rotting
   - Windows boarded up
   - Graffiti.
   (*2 marks*)

7. 'Greenfield' has connotations of something natural and of open spaces, whereas the housing scheme is run-down and depressing.
(*2 marks*)

8. The people who had designed the scheme and who allocated tenants to houses there would never have to experience these living conditions themselves.
(*2 marks*)

9. These features suggest that the people who live in the bungalows wish to keep themselves to themselves (net curtains) and are frightened that residents of the housing estate may break in.
(*2 marks*)

10. He is always ready with a sarcastic reply (e.g. 'I just didn't know there was a clairvoyant on the premises') or any other valid point, backed up with evidence.
(*2 marks*)

11. Recognition of personification (1 mark); explanation of effectiveness – e.g. the trolleys resemble women who live on the estate gossiping about their neighbours.
(*2 marks*)

12. Possibilities include:

    - Contrasting sentence lengths
    - Parenthesis in paragraph one
    - Question form in paragraph three
    - Use of direct speech
    - Sentence structures in lines 70–74 reflect Rebus's train of thought
    - Last paragraph (line 75) consists simply of two words.
    (*2 marks*)

    Total: 25 marks

JOURNALISM (1): THE CAT CAME BACK QUESTIONS (Page 30)

1. Lines 13–14: the styling of the front end echoes the traditional look of earlier Jaguars ('retro-look styling') with 'beautifully curving wings and flared wheel arches'.
(*2 marks*)

2. The audio-cassette holder (line 23).
(*1 mark*)

3. Possibilities include:

   - Wood inserts in the dashboard
   - Twin headlamps
   - The car has a three litre V6 engine
   - There are cup-holders fitted under the armrest.
   (*3 marks*)

4. Possibilities include:

   - The air-intake grille is smooth and perfectly formed
   - The cup-holders are discreet
   - The badge on the cassette holder resembles the 'flashing insignia from an arcade pinball machine'
   - The engine growls like an alley cat.
   (*2 marks*)

5. (i) People whose hair has become whiter, not because it has been dyed, but because they are growing old. *(2 marks)*

   (ii) Line 38: 'Travelling in style, guvnor.' The term 'guvnor' might be how a chauffeur addresses the businessman he is driving, thus suggesting something about the type of person likely to have such a car. *(2 marks)*

6. (i) (a) *Jargon*: technical language, as in line 33: '3-litre AJ–V6 engine'; terms such as 'torque'. *(1 mark)*

   (b) *Colloquial language*: e.g. line 4: 'That's the new Jag!' *(1 mark)*

   (c) *Formal language*: e.g. lines 17–18: 'Here we must abide by the Euro pedestrian-protection rule'; lines 29–30: 'Supreme looks are matched by exquisitely refined mechanics.' *(1 mark)*

   (d) *Hyperbole*: some of the comparisons made involve exaggeration, such as lines 31–32 ('There's more energy . . . a penguin's belly on ice.') *(1 mark)*

   (ii) Many possibilities. Examples of hyperbole probably offer the greatest scope for commentary. Example of a good answer:

   'There's more energy expended flicking a Subbuteo player than changing gear' is effective as it creates an impression of how effortless the car is to drive, since flicking a Subbuteo player merely involves a light movement of the finger. *(2 marks)*

7. (i) Examples in lines 31–32 and line 36. Pupils should not repeat the same example used in a previous answer. *(2 marks)*

   (ii) 'The onset of mid-life winter' (lines 10–11) metaphorically refers to old age. Comparisons to women in lines 39–42 are metaphorical, as are references to 'king' and 'pretender' in lines 11–12. *(2 marks)*

8. Relevant references include: line 16 ('Top Cat badge'); line 25 ('Amazonian royal'); line 36 ('kitten', 'alley cat'); line 42 ('figure-hugging cat suit'); line 43 ('Miaow'). Good answers will not only pick up these references but will comment on the similarities between the cat and the car – e.g. speed, gracefulness, latent power, etc. *(3 marks)*

Total: 25 marks

JOURNALISM (2): 'A SUDDEN, SERIOUS BRUSH WITH MORTALITY' QUESTIONS (Pages 32–33)

1. Real life is haphazard/untidy/disorganised, etc. (each sport has a clearly structured framework/rules, etc.)

   Alternative point: sport provides a forum in which the best aspects of human nature – courage, single-minded effort – can flourish. *(2 marks)*

2. Frivolity. *(1 mark)*

3. Unexpectedly finding oneself in a dangerous and life-threatening situation. *(2 marks)*

4. It makes the person question his or her priorities, and realise that 'what really matters is not sport but life itself'. *(2 marks)*

5. One mark for each of the following:

   • Others had questioned his character and behaviour ('temperament'), in particular his ability to keep going ('tenacity')

   • He experienced self-doubt

   • A series of mechanical difficulties with his racing car. *(3 marks)*

6. Lines 25–7: 'a harrowing rendezvous with the grim reaper'. *(1 mark)*

7. He only experienced three broken ribs (1 mark) when two other people died (1 mark). (2 *marks*)

8. 'Composed, dignified deportment'; 'genuinely inspirational' (whole phrase or single words acceptable).
   (2 *marks*)

9. (a) Simile (or possibly hyperbole). (1 *mark*)

   (b) Keeping the car on the road on this racing circuit is an extremely delicate and difficult operation.
   (2 *marks*)

10. Line 35: 'Coulthard handled the Mercedes McLaren like she was painted to the road'. (1 *mark*)

11. Paraphrase of: 'The crippling ghosts of self-doubt were ruthlessly exorcised' (e.g. he has faced up to his inner fears and doubts and has triumphed over them) or 'emerged reinvigorated and tougher' (e.g. he has become stronger and has gained new life and energy). (2 *marks*)

12. He will not let success go to his head; will not become proud and arrogant. (2 *marks*)

13. (a) Reinvigorated.

    (b) Taboo. (2 *marks*)

Total: 25 marks

FANTASY (1): THE HOWLER QUESTIONS (Page 36)

1. The 'enchanted ceiling' can change to reflect weather conditions. (1 *mark*)

2. Neville Longbottom's character is:
   - 'Cheerful': happy/optimistic, etc.
   - 'Accident prone': unfortunate things seemed to keep happening to him. (2 *marks*)

3. A Howler is a message, which is delivered in an envelope; however, the message is delivered not in a written form but in the voice and tone of the person who sent it. (2 *marks*)

4. She uses block capitals. (1 *mark*)

5. (a) All the sentences are run together with commas instead of being separated by full stops. (1 *mark*)

   (b) It imitates how Mrs Weasley pours out her angry message in a breathless, non-stop fashion. (1 *mark*)

   (c) '. . . stealing the car! I wouldn't have been surprised if they'd expelled you! You wait till I get hold of you. I don't suppose you stopped to think what your father and I went through when we saw it had gone?' (Full stops or exclamation marks as appropriate.) (2 *marks*)

6. Possibilities include: 'you wait till I get hold of you'; 'die of shame'; 'we didn't bring you up to behave like this'; 'absolutely disgusted'. (2 *marks*)

7. (a) stealing the car. (1 *mark*)

   (b) Reference to lines 9–11 '. . . she was still disapproving of the way they had arrived'. (1 *mark*)

   (c) (i) Ron slipped down very low in his chair; his face went bright red.
       (ii) Harry pretended he could not hear the message; the noise was hurting his eardrums. (4 *marks*)

   (d) The shame that their behaviour has brought upon her. Answer should include a suitable reference (e.g. line 45, 54 or 61). (2 *marks*)

8. 'Ringing' refers to something loud whereas 'silence' is an absence of sound. Two opposites are placed side by side (oxymoron). (2 *marks*)

9. Line 67: 'a ringing silence fell'. This short sentence is well placed after the noisy scene of the arrival of the Howler as it creates a dramatic pause. The reader is left wondering how everyone in the hall will react, and the embarrassment of Ron and Harry is highlighted. *(2 marks)*

Total: 25 marks

FANTASY (2) IN THE RETIRING ROOM QUESTIONS (Pages 39–40)

1. Gloss on 'taking care to keep to one side'; 'out of sight of the kitchen'. Lyra looks back at the kitchen to check no one is watching before she steps up on the dais. *(2 marks)*

2. 'What little light there was'; 'little light'; '(in the) gloom'. *(1 mark)*

3. It is physically high, being on a dais/platform (Lyra had to 'step up'); it is also grander with gold and silver place settings and more luxurious seats. Important people sit there – it has the Master's chair. *(2 marks)*

4. He was 'currently' in the form of a moth, suggesting he was sometimes something else. His dark brown colour 'so as not to show up in the darkness' suggests he is able to change his colour for camouflage. *(2 marks)*

5. (a) Metaphor. *(1 mark)*

   (b) Explanation with some reference to water/firework image. *(1 mark)*

6. Lyra had never seen it before, so it must be exclusive; women were not allowed in; only special people ('scholars and their guests') were admitted; maids were not even allowed in to clean it; only the Butler was special enough to look after it. *(2 marks)*

7. (a) They indulge themselves in luxury; pamper/treat themselves. *(1 mark)*

   (b) Reference to two of: elegant furniture ('polished rosewood'; 'leather armchairs'); drinks ('decanters and glasses); expensive equipment ('silver smoking-mill'). (Quotations alone = ½ marks. No marks if (a) is wrong.) *(2 marks)*

8. Suitable explanation, e.g., it builds up suspense, suggesting she may be caught. *(2 marks)*

9. Lyra cannot see the speaker; she hears but does not see the Master. *(1 mark)*

10. (a) With effort/difficulty. *(1 mark)*

    (b) Reference to Master's age and his movements being 'stiff and slow'. (No marks if (a) is wrong.) *(2 marks)*

11. Poisoning or drugging the wine. *(1 mark)*

12. Lyra is more playful 'flicked the glass'; Pan is more serious: 'You're not taking this seriously'. He is more cautious, nervous and careful: 'whispers'; and responsible: he tells her to 'behave yourself'. Lyra does accept Pan's warning, although she mocks his caution: 'Stop fussing.' Pan is more nervous and wants to leave: 'Can we go?'. Lyra is more daring; she wants to stay and explore: 'Don't be silly! I want to look around'. Pan is panicking: 'bristling with anxiety'; Lyra enjoys the challenge: 'pleasantly excited'. *(4 marks)*

Total: 25 marks

CHILDHOOD IN FICTION (1): MAN AND BOY QUESTIONS (Pages 43–44)

1. Pat's formal clothes underlined how much of a baby he still was. Harry had expected that dressing him like an adult would have made him look older. *(2 marks)*

2. He had thought Pat was beautiful when he was a young infant, but he wondered if every parent instinctively saw beauty in their own baby, whether the baby really was beautiful or not. *(2 marks)*

3. (a) Phrases: 'wasn't smiling'; 'pale and silent'; 'struggling to stop his chin trembling'; 'his bottom lip sticking out'. Single words: 'pale', 'silent', 'struggling', 'trembling' (Any two). *(1 mark)*

   (b) Answers dependent on two expressions chosen, but should include references to ideas contrasting with these expressions, such as happy, cheerful, smiling, chatty, rosy-cheeked, relaxed, composed and calm. *(2 marks)*

4. It stresses that it was an important moment in both their lives; it throws a spotlight on the moment of leaving home and makes it stand out as important. *(2 marks)*

5. 'Swarms' is associated with large numbers of unpleasant things, especially stinging insects. It suggests the number of children was frighteningly large, and makes them seem dangerous and intimidating.
   'Tribe' is usually used for a group of savages. It is comical when used for small children only three feet in height, but suggests they are wild and uncivilised. *(2 marks)*

6. 'Marched' has military associations, and is used *ironically* or *humorously* to describe the infants' parents being led to the classroom.
   It gives an impression of officious or fussy regimentation, with the parents being ordered about as if they were in the army or being sent to prison. *(2 marks)*

7. (a) Usually only mothers would be present, and so she would not need to mention daddies. She added it to include Harry's unusual situation. *(1 mark)*

   (b) EITHER: he might feel *better*, as he felt included and accepted in the group; OR he might feel *worse*, as she was drawing attention to his pitiable situation as a single father whose wife had left him. *(1 mark)*

8. Both Pat and he were embarking on new stages of their lives, and Harry realised that by the time it was over he would be rather old, which was quite a depressing thought. OR He was sad at the thought that the carefree days of staying at home and watching videos with Pat were now over. *(2 marks)*

9. (a) Chaperone; someone who is a companion to a younger person and who also watches over them. *(1 mark)*

   (b) The expression 'look after the new boys and girls' suggests the volunteers will be caring for and acting as friends to the new children; 'I'm going to take care of you' shows Peggy is going to be responsible for Pat; 'took his hand and led him into the classroom' illustrates the idea of a chaperone who guides and accompanies a younger person. *(1 mark)*

10. Possible answers include:
    sadness, as Harry felt Pat had forgotten him already and was moving on; *relief*, as Harry could see Pat was clearly going to be happy; *jealousy*, as Pat had transferred his affections to the little girl; *happiness*, as he felt glad Pat had found a friend; *pride*, as Pat was confident and a credit to him as a parent. *(2 marks)*

11. Possible pieces of evidence include:
    Harry being 'seized by a moment of panic' shows that he too feels apprehension at the two of them being parted; Harry's saying, 'I could lose him in here', shows his concern at being separated from Pat, while his irrational fear of losing him 'for ever' gives the impression he is empathising with Pat; 'I took Pat's clammy hand' shows their physical closeness, and Harry's desire to give Pat moral support, while his noticing the clamminess of Pat's hand is observant, showing his concern for him; the repeated use of the pronoun 'we' shows Harry sees himself and Pat as a pair and indicates how close the two of them are. *(4 marks)*

Total: 25 marks

CHILDHOOD IN FICTION (2): I KNOW THIS MUCH IS TRUE QUESTIONS (Pages 48–49)

1. It might seem ironic as going back to school would not usually seem like a cause for celebration ('festival') or to be a source of 'fun'. *(1 mark)*

2. The 'nice' driver talks to the children and jokes with them; he pretends to do tricks and gives them sweets: 'pulls candy out of your ears'; he says goodbye to them in a jokey way: 'See you later, alligator'; he is good humoured: 'laughs'. *(2 marks)*

3. (a) 'Crabby' means bad-tempered. The lady is refusing to allow children in to the picture show as they are too young, showing she is strict and severe. She 'yells' at the children showing she is irritable. *(2 marks)*

   (b) Grouchy. *(1 mark)*

4. By marking the 'X' on their hand he can tell who has already had a free pencil box, so that no one can try to get more than one. *(1 mark)*

5. They sit near the middle of the cinema, not at the front, as their mother thinks that would be bad for their eyes. The mother sits in between the two boys, presumably so that she can control their behaviour more easily. *(2 marks)*

6. Dominick is counting the cartoons as they are shown on his fingers, and he realises they have only shown eight, not the ten they were promised, as he has only counted as far as his eighth finger. *(2 marks)*

7. She is afraid the boys will copy their dangerous or messy antics, such as poking fingers into eyes or falling onto cakes. *(1 mark)*

8. (a) The 'bad' children have flattened their popcorn boxes and started throwing them in the air. The shapes of the boxes reflected on the screen look like flying bats. This reminds Dominick of what he knows about bats. *(2 marks)*

   (b) Suitable examples:
   (lines 80–87) *The Three Stooges* is set in a school called West Point → his own school → the time a dog came into his school classroom (lines 88–91) The children who are firing pellets → cowboys under fire → his favourite cowboy shows such as *The Rifleman*. *(1 mark)*

9. Line 35 – represents the sound made by the cartoon character, Roadrunner (onomatopoeia);
   Line 46 – direct speech, repeating a catchphrase from a cartoon;
   Line 72 – represents the sound made by the pellets (onomatopoeia);
   Line 77 – represents the sound of Thomas sucking the eraser (onomatopoeia);
   Lines 80–81 – Title of film;
   Line 91 – Titles of TV Westerns. *(2 marks)*

10. There is some jealousy and sibling rivalry, especially on Dominick's side. Dominick insists on pulling the stop cord in the bus 'because Thomas did it last time'. He also feels he has the right to disobey his mother and open the pencil box since Thomas has got away with it: 'if Thomas can, so can I'. However, Thomas is more infantile, and sucks his eraser, while Dominick is naughtier and 'boings' his. Dominick is bolder – he is the one who shouts back to the bus driver. He argues with his mother 'Why not?'. Thomas is more timid and needs his mother's reassurance about the new teacher, he is scared of 'getting stomach aches thinking about her'. Dominick doesn't seem to feel this way. The twins are alike in that both enjoy the same things, and laugh at *The Three Stooges*. *(4 marks)*

11. *Sentence structure*: Many sentences are very short giving the impression of a child's limited expression. 'We're on the city bus'. Most are simple in structure with a subject – verb word order 'Ma's scared'. There are few subordinate clauses which suggests the simple thoughts of a child. Sometimes the grammar is wrong: 'Her and this other lady . . .'. Some minor sentences are used: 'Just sitting there'.
    Ideas: Child's curiosity is shown in wondering how the 'grouchy' driver lost his thumb, or why the 'crabby' lady is bad-tempered. Simple black-and-white view of things, e.g. 'nice bus driver', 'bad kids', is childish. Simple commentary on Thomas's sucking of the eraser 'which is stupid'. Interests are childish: cowboy movies, bats, the dog in the classroom. Sense of humour is immature – as in plot of *The Three Stooges*. He is surprised to learn the tallest man is not the boss.
    Word choice: Very simple words, frequently monosyllables, and expressions are used throughout: 'I didn't

want to but I did.' Childish slang is used: 'wiseguys'. Descriptions are simple and also use slang: 'crabby' 'a snotty rich lady'. Some words such as 'Ma' indicate a child. His enjoyment of onomatopoeia is childish: 'boings' 'ping'. Language is colloquial and includes abbreviations such as 'he's' and 'it's'.

Point of view/perspective: Dominick is fascinated by the deformed hand of the bus driver, and can't stop looking at it. He is typically observant, noting physical peculiarities such as the 'bulgy eyes' of the ticket man. Adults seem very big to him: the usher is described as 'very, very tall'. Dominick frequently quotes his mother, as if he sees her as a source of knowledge: 'Ma says . . .' Dominick has to obey his mother and sit where she sits and ask permission to buy popcorn. His view of Thomas's sucking the eraser is simply 'it is stupid', whereas an adult would see deeper significance in this.

Descriptive language: Simple, non technical language is used 'bulgy-eyed man'. Simple expressions without subtlety reflect a child's limited powers of description: 'grouchy', 'crabby'. His expression relates to familiar things: the dog has a 'smiley' face. The frequent use of 'and' in the description of the dog in line 86 is typical of a child. *(4 marks)*

Total: 25 marks

SNOW IN THE SUBURBS QUESTIONS (Pages 53–54)

1. Simile: 'every fork like a white web-foot': the way the snow fills up the gaps between the twigs resembles the skin/membranes on the feet of a duck or similar creature.

   Metaphor: 'the palings are glued together like a wall': the snow fills in the gaps in the wooden fence so that it appears solid.

   Metaphor: 'fleecy fall': comparison between the snow and a sheep's wool – similarities of whiteness, texture, etc.

   (In each case, one mark for quotation and one mark for comment.) *(4 marks)*

2. (a) Bent every twig with it. *(1 mark)*

   (b) Every street and pavement mute/there is no waft of wind. *(1 mark)*

3. 'Meandering' means wandering about with no fixed destination in mind; the snow floats down gently in a similar way. *(2 marks)*

4. (a) Alliteration. *(1 mark)*

   (b) 'Waft' means to float or drift gently through the air; the alliteration emphasises the calmness of the scene, and the manner in which the snow is falling down. *(1 mark)*

5. Four of the following for one mark each: He alights on the tree/a large lump of snow falls on him from above/it covers his eyes/it knocks him off balance/and nearly buries him ('inurns')/it starts off a further avalanche of snow. *(4 marks)*

6. Two of the following for one mark each: it is hungry/it is cold/it has not been well-looked after ('wide-eyed and thin')/it does not expect to find any food or shelter ('with feeble hope'). *(2 marks)*

7. Marks could be gained in various ways, but evidence and quotation must always be included.

   Example of a good four-mark answer:

   The first part of the poem builds up a feeling of peacefulness by describing how the snow thoroughly covers the whole scene and spreads a calm, quiet atmosphere: 'every street and pavement mute'. Verse two introduces some humour, as the poet is amused by the smallness of the sparrow compared to the huge lump of snow that falls on him. A sadder note is introduced towards the end, reminding the reader that some creatures find it hard to survive in winter conditions, such as the 'black cat . . . wide-eyed and thin'. *(4 marks)*

   Total: 20 marks

HAMNAVOE MARKET QUESTIONS (Pages 55–56)

1. The exclamation mark indicates strong feelings. It suggests happiness, excitement and delight at freedom from school. *(2 marks)*

2. 'A cheapjack' or travelling pedlar would be typical of the past; 'swing-boats' are old-fashioned fairground amusements; 'apples and ginger beer' are old-fashioned refreshments; 'the blind fiddler' and boxing are entertainments from a past age; shillings are old coins no longer in use. *(2 marks)*

3. The writer had quickly spent all his money on these things, and so it was as if the shillings had lost the battle to stay in his pocket. *(2 marks)*

4. The narrator is pleased with his prize and values the 'diamond' locket, perhaps believing it to be valuable; the reader knows it will actually be glass and quite worthless. *(2 marks)*

5. They were small and rounded in shape; they were close together, in the way mushrooms are often grouped; they had sprung up overnight, as mushrooms do. *(2 marks)*

6. It looks at the building from the drunk man's point of view, where everything is unsteady; it suggests the whole village is happy and rather drunk with celebrating at the market. *(2 marks)*

7. The full stops after 'hoof' and 'lingered' create pauses which slow up the line, suggesting the slow setting of the sun. The use of enjambment in 'It fell/On a nest of flares' ends the description with a rush, as if darkness suddenly fell. The abruptness of the monosyllable 'fell' contrasts with the longer word 'lingered'. *(2 marks)*

8. References to 'yellow', 'goldfish' and 'golden' suggest brightness. The coloured balloons are a colourful image as balloons are always in primary colours. References to precious things suggest sparkle: 'diamond'; 'crystal'. Shillings are silver in colour, and they are said to be 'bright', as if new and shiny. The imagery of light and the heavens in 'high as the moon' and 'the sun whirled a golden hoof' suggests brightness. *(4 marks)*

9. It is effective as the reference to the horse 'Old Madge our mare' returns to the beginning of the poem where the children are arriving by gig. The reference to 'homed' suggests the joy of going home after a happy day out. The description of the night as 'black as a bottle of ink' contrasts with the brightness of the day which has just gone, and suggests all good things come to an end. *(2 marks)*

Total: 20 marks

'OUT, OUT – ' QUESTIONS (Page 58)

1. (a) 'Snarled' is onomatopoeic and suggests the low growling noise made when the teeth of the saw bite into the wood; 'rattled' indicates the loud, vibrating noise when the cutting is finished and the saw runs on without the teeth engaging. *(2 marks)*

   (b) A wild/hungry animal. *(1 mark)*

   (c) It indicates the repetitive nature of the task; It builds up suspense with a series of climaxes followed by an anticlimax. *(1 mark)*

2. It is an anticlimax. *(1 mark)*

3. Finish work for the day. *(1 mark)*

4. (a) The boy's sister came to tell him his supper was ready. Momentarily distracted, he allowed his hand to drift on to the teeth of the saw, which almost severed it from his arm. *(2 marks)*

   (b) It is an effective personification. The saw appears to have an evil mind of its own and its idea of supper is the boy's arm which it fixes its teeth into. There is a grim humour in the alternative idea of 'supper'. *(2 marks)*

5. The dash after 'then' creates a sudden pause, which indicates his pulse becoming irregular and makes the watcher 'take fright'. The short sentences build up tension. The single words with the dashes in between: 'little – less – nothing! – ' mimic the fluttering of his heart-beat which dies out on the word 'nothing'. The exclamation mark emphasises the shock of this sudden heart failure. *(4 marks)*

6. In line 18, the exclamation mark lets us know something dreadful has happened to the hand. It raises the emotional level of the verse and creates tension.
   In line 26, the exclamation mark is used more conventionally to indicate the boy crying out, but also indicates that the speaker is highly emotional. *(4 marks)*

7. Many possible interpretations, such as indignation/anger/resentment at life continuing as if the boy's death was of little importance; resignation/calm/acceptance of reality, showing admiration that people can and do carry on in the face of such tragedy. *(2 marks)*

Total: 20 marks

POEM FOR MY SISTER QUESTIONS (Pages 59–60)

1. To pretend she was a grown-up; to copy an admired older sister. *(1 mark)*

2. She walks proudly, with a swagger, as if she is a model on a catwalk. *(2 marks)*

3. The shoes are actually much too big for her; she just likes to pretend she is big enough to fit them. It adds a humorous touch. *(1 mark)*

4. Possible examples: 'spindle-thin' or 'her spindle-thin twelve-year-old legs': this is humorous as the picture of very skinny legs ending in over-large shoes is comic, with the fact that the little girl is so proud of her legs adding to the humour.
   'Wobbles' or 'wobbles on their high heels' is funny as she is obviously unused to high heels and we wonder if she will fall over, although she claims the shoes 'fit her perfectly'. *(2 marks)*

5. Sentence structure: The sentence is long, divided up into a large number of short and slightly longer phrases which mimic the series of jumps to be made in a game of hopscotch.
   Rhythm: The rhythm speeds up in the compound words such as 'hops-and-skips' which mimics the irregular hopping movements of the game. The monosyllables also contribute to this jerky effect.
   Punctuation: The commas between the phrases mimic the pauses between jumps which occur in the game; the hyphens in the numerous compound words reinforce this effect. *(3 marks)*

6. Neat; quick; never-missing; competent. *(2 marks)*

7. Parallel constructions are used in these lines, with only two words changing, like → try and watch → warn. The tone in verse two is relaxed and happy. The speaker is passive, simply observing and admiring her sister's confidence and expertise; in verse three the tone becomes more serious and anxious, with a note of uncertainty in 'try'. The speaker is taking a more active role in wishing to 'warn' her sister and hoping to protect her. *(3 marks)*

8. It puts the feet out of shape; it creates hard growths of skin; it hardens the skin in places. *(2 marks)*

9. In my position/situation. *(1 mark)*

10. Unsuitable shoes: unwise life choices/harmful or hurtful experiences in life; my own distorted feet . . . hard skin: psychological harm, the trauma, pain and unhappiness that arise from such bad experiences; surefooted: doing the right things, not making mistakes which will harm her life.
    Sensibly shod: making the right choices which will enhance her life. *(4 marks)*

11. The sisters have a close and loving relationship. Younger sister is allowed to 'try' older sister's shoes, showing she wishes to be like her, and which shows older sister is indulgent. Older sister enjoys watching her and finds her amusing as she 'wobbles'. Older sister likes spending time with the younger, watching her

at her games, like 'hopscotch'. Words such as 'admire', 'competent' and 'neat' reveal a positive and loving attitude. The last verse shows the older sister is protective of the younger as she tries to 'warn' her away from unsuitable things which might harm her. She has had bad experiences which she does not want her sister to have; she does not want to see her 'in my shoes'. *(4 marks)*

Total: 25 marks

HEATHER ALE QUESTIONS (Pages 64-65)

1. A cheerful and positive mood. This is continued in the idea of the brewing of a wonderful drink whose potency induces a euphoric stupor. The notion of the ale being 'sweeter far than honey' makes it almost magical, and the word 'blessed' gives the drinking of it an almost religious significance. A sense of security is suggested in the 'dwellings underground'. The phrase 'for days and days' suggests a carefree existence without worries or responsibilities, devoted to pleasure. *(4 marks)*

2. The mood becomes dark and tragic. The idea of a ruthless 'fell' king hunting down and killing the Picts contrasts with the relaxed mood of the previous verse. The king's attitude to his enemies is also shocking. The Picts are hunted down like animals. 'Roes' compares them to timid, gentle deer. Their panic is evident in the phrase 'as they fled' and shows that no mercy was given by the king. The fact the Picts' bodies are 'strewed' suggests the large number of deaths and the disrespectful way their bodies were treated, left lying unburied. The word choice is menacing with the repetition of 'hunted' and the doom-laded word 'smote'. The fact the mountain is 'red' suggests the blood of the Picts. *(4 marks)*

3. 'Red was the heather bell'; 'red moorland'. Red suggests the colour of the heather, but also has connotations of bloodshed and danger. 'Black was his brow' suggests that the king was dark haired, but also implies a frowning, severe expression. It suggests his evil intentions towards the Picts. *(4 marks)*

4. (a) They were small in stature. *(1 mark)*

   (b) It arouses sympathy, as you might feel for a child. *(1 mark)*

5. 'Sat high' suggests the king's arrogance. He is physically higher than the Picts and he is looking down on them both literally and metaphorically. 'Little men' suggests he sees them not just as physically small but as insignificant and unimportant. The fact that the Picts 'looked at the king' suggests they are not intimidated. To look someone in the eye is a gesture of defiance. *(4 marks)*

6. Since he is old, life has become particularly precious and he is not willing to sacrifice it to keep the secret of the ale. He no longer bothers about his honour or values it as a young person might do. He asks them to kill his son first, claiming he would feel embarrassed to betray the secret, while his son, who does value honour over life, is looking on in contempt. *(3 marks)*

7. He believes his son would not have had the courage to withstand torture, but would have eventually yielded the secret. He knows that he himself has the willpower to keep the secret and never give in, whatever methods of torture are applied. *(2 marks)*

8. The Picts appear to be self-indulgent characters who spend most of their time drinking, and show little evidence of the strong moral fibre, revealed by the Old Pict. *(1 mark)*

9. *Setting, weather and landscape*: 'Bonny bells of heather' creates an idyllic scene. However, the frequent references to the 'red' of the flowers suggests bloodshed. The sight of the 'red heather' mentioned in verse 7 perhaps strengthens the old Pict's desire for revenge. The reference to summer in verses 3 and 4 and the description of how the 'bees hummed' remind us of the happy land in verse 1, but it seems ironic here in view of the horrible events. The final scenes set on the 'giddy brink' of the cliffs are very evocative and visually stimulating.

Direct Speech: Throughout the poem this brings dramatic realism. The words of the king in verse 6 build his character as arrogant and unsympathetic when he calls the Picts 'vermin'. The sycophantic wheedling of the old man – 'a word in the royal ear' – builds suspense as he pretends to be ingratiating himself with the king and even pleading for his son to be killed. The contrast between the tone here and the fearless defiance of his final taunting words is very effective: 'Now in vain is the torture'. Direct speech is frequently used in traditional ballads, a genre to which this poem belongs.

The use of techniques involving sound: Alliteration is used effectively to make phrases stand out e.g., 'the dying and the dead' in verse 2. Here the emphatic 'd' sound intensifies the sense. In verse 4, 'black was his brow' achieves a similar ominous effect with the heavy 'b' sounds. Onomatopoeia is used in verse 4: 'the bees hummed'. This pleasant sound in nature contrasts ironically with the horror in human events. The sea which 'rumbled' below in verse 7 suggests stormy and dangerous water and builds up tension.

The verses are each in the form of a double quatrain with an abcb rhyme scheme. This is typical of a ballad rhyme scheme which is suitable for this narrative poem. Each line has three stressed syllables which lends itself to very simple sentence structures, again giving the impression of a ballad, a simple story set in verse. *(6 marks)*

Total: 30 marks

PART TWO: WRITING SKILLS

PUNCTUATION (1) For Practice (Pages 67–68)

(a) I had before me a choice of route. I chose a ridge which made an angle with the one I was on, and so would put a deep glen between me and my enemies. The exercise had warmed my blood. I was beginning to enjoy myself amazingly. As I went, I breakfasted on the dusty remnants of the ginger biscuits. I knew very little about the country. I hadn't a notion what I was going to do. I trusted to the strength of my legs, but I was well aware that those behind me would be familiar with the lie of the land, and that my ignorance would be a heavy handicap. I saw in front of me a sea of hills, rising very high toward the south, but northwards breaking down into broad ridges which separated wide and shallow dales. That seemed as good a direction to take as any other.

(b) As I said these words, I perceived in the gloom a figure which stole from behind a clump of trees near me. I stood fixed, gazing intently. I could not be mistaken. A flash of lightning illuminated the object and revealed its shape plainly to me. Its gigantic stature and the deformity of its aspect instantly informed me that it was the wretch, the filthy demon, to whom I had given life. What did he there? Could he be the murderer of my brother? No sooner did that idea cross my imagination than I became convinced of its truth. My teeth chattered. I was forced to lean against a tree for support. The figure passed me quickly and I lost it in the gloom.

PUNCTUATION (2) (Pages 68–69)

(a) It was early in the morning. Making my way towards the house, I saw the front door was open. I hurried to my father's room as I wanted to discover how much he knew, or whether he knew anything about what had happened last night. As soon as I went into the room it was clear from his face that he already knew all about it and I wondered what I should say.

(b) A poem that I liked was 'Listen tae the Teacher' by Nancy Nicolson, which is about a small boy being confused whether to speak in Scots or English. The poem uses both Scots language and standard English. In the poem, the Scots language gives a rhythm which makes the poem like a song, and the poem sounds more effective when it is set to music. It also has a chorus which is entertaining.

PUNCTUATION (3) (Page 70)

(c) <u>Faults</u>:

- Comma splices: line 5 (after area); line 13 (after a crime); line 14 (after the crime); line 15 (after fault); line 21 (after wrong).

- Poor style: repetition of 'I' at the beginning of sentences in lines 1 and 3; and again in lines 14 and 15. Repetition of 'and' in the final sentence. In line 8, 'at first' is unnecessary.
- Examples of clumsy expression: 'with two of the other escapees caught' (lines 9–10); 'my so called friend Robbie's fault' (lines 15–16); 'and it wasn't me' (line 20).
- Changing the word order in lines 12–13 would throw more effective emphasis on the length of the prison sentence. Changing the word order in the final sentence would create a more effective cliff-hanger as the police dogs come closer.
- A new paragraph could be inserted at line 11: 'I had been jailed . . .' where the flashback is introduced, and again at line 20 where the story returns to the present.
- Short sentences could be introduced for variety.

<u>Alternative version:</u>

I ran through the darkened streets, in and out of alleyways with my coat flying behind me. Hearing the shouting of the men as their dogs searched the surrounding area, I stopped and listened more closely. Then I moved on. The escape had turned out to be harder than I thought it would be, and with two of the other escapees having been caught there was not much chance of me surviving the night.

Five years before, I had been jailed for committing a crime in which I had not been involved. It had all been the fault of my so-called friend, Robbie. He had been the one who told them everything, but what he hadn't told them was that he was the one who had done it and not me.

Finally I reached the field where we had arranged to meet if anything went wrong. No one was there. I climbed a tree and waited a while, but no one came along. In the distance I could hear the police dogs barking.

PUNCTUATION (4) (Page 73)

Four days after these curious incidents, a funeral started from Canterville Chase. The hearse was drawn by a black horse which carried a great tuft of ostrich-plumes on its head. The leaden coffin was covered by a rich purple pall on which was embroidered in gold the Canterville coat-of-arms. By the side of the hearse and the coaches walked the servants who carried lighted torches, making the whole procession wonderfully impressive. Lord Canterville, the chief mourner who had come up specially from Wales, sat in the first carriage along with little Virginia. In the last carriage came Mrs Umney. As she had been frightened by the ghost for more than fifty years of her life, she had a right to see the last of him.

PUNCTUATION (5) (Page 74)

There is no doubt that the Internet is revolutionising the way we do business. The existence of email makes communication much quicker. In addition, businesses can make contact with many more potential customers than before. Furthermore, it is now possible to order almost any goods, from books to groceries, over the Internet. However, this does not suit everyone. Some potential customers find unwanted emails as annoying as the junk mail than comes through their letter boxes. Similarly, many people prefer to see what they are buying first. Nevertheless, internet shopping is something that everyone will have to get used to as it is certain to grow in the next few years.

PUNCTUATION (6) (Page 75)

There is one reason above all others why Versailles is worth a pilgrimage to see: everything is on so gigantic a scale. Nothing is small; nothing is cheap. The statues are all large; the palace is grand; the park covers a fair-sized country; the avenues are interminable. Some people have been very critical of Louis XIV: he is accused of spending two hundred millions of dollars in creating this marvellous park, when bread was so scarce with some of his subjects; but I have forgiven him now.

WORD CHOICE (1) Avoiding overused words (Pages 76-79)

Pages 76-77 Get
I entered through a side door which was hanging from its hinges. It made a long eerie creak as I pushed it open. I heard the sound of breaking glass and laughing. As I moved closer the passage grew narrower. Eventually I had to crawl. When I emerged into the open I reached the balcony of the warehouse. I could see that the two groups of men in the courtyard below were preparing to exchange briefcases. There were handshakes all round. Everything seemed to be taking so long that I wished I'd bought some food at the shop at the corner of

the street, for it seemed like I was going to be stuck there all night. It was then that I realised what was going to happen: from my high-up vantage point I could see one of the men slowly drawing a gun out of his jacket pocket.

(i)   We just managed to catch the train two minutes before it left.
(ii)   I managed to arrange for a glazier to come and fix the window.
(iii) By changing jobs she ended up earning a much higher salary.
(iv)   I'll have to purchase/fetch/obtain another tin of paint to finish off the decorating.
(v)   The policeman grabbed hold of/seized the thief who was trying to escape through the back window.

Page 77

A	B
Get back	return
Get across (information)	convey
Get at	annoy
Get over (e.g. a difficulty)	surmount
Get by	survive
Get round	evade
Get out of	escape
Get off	disembark
Get ready	prepare

A lot
(i)   On the first morning at my new school I met many new people I had never seen before.
(ii)   I had considerable difficulty trying to work out the answers to the Maths questions.
(iii) He gave me several different explanations for what he had done, but it was clear that these were just excuses.

Page 78 So
(i)   As our car had been in an accident the garage provided us with a courtesy car.
OR The garage provided us with a courtesy car because our car had been in an accident.
(ii)   He left the house at 7 am so that he could be there in plenty of time.
(iii) We are going to hold a jumble sale because/as extra funds are needed if the club is to continue.

Word Choice (2) Expanding your range of vocabulary (Pages 80–82)

Page 80

(a)

Group 1	Group 2
1. J	1. B
2. G	2. F
3. F	3. I
4. H	4. H
5. A	5. E
6. E	6. D
7. D	7. C
8. C	8. A
9. B	9. J
10. I	10. G

Page 81

(b)

(i)   Although he was usually a very friendly person, he behaved towards the visitors in a rather <u>inhospitable</u> way

(ii) The behaviour of the <u>notorious</u> criminal had clearly been <u>culpable</u> but when the crime was discovered he showed a very <u>penitent</u> attitude.

(iii) The Member of Parliament was asked several times to explain his Party's views on the issue, but his answers were <u>inconsistent</u>.

(iv) At school he seemed very <u>inhibited</u>, rarely mixing with people or taking part in anything, but once he started working he developed into a much more <u>gregarious</u> person.

(v) Brian's enthusiasm for the team was so great that it was bordering on the <u>fanatical</u>.

(vi) The vet was shocked when he heard of the man's <u>callous</u> treatment of the dog.

(vii) When questioned the boy could offer no <u>rational</u> explanation of why he had broken the window.

Page 82

(a)

1. D
2. H
3. J
4. E
5. F
6. G
7. I
8. C
9. B
10. A

Word Choice (3) Words that people often confuse (Pages 82–86)

(i) Once she reaches the age of seventy my gran will be <u>eligible</u> for a free television licence.
(ii) The house was so quiet that I could almost <u>hear</u> myself <u>breathe</u>.
(iii) My neighbour was so fed up with the state of the road that he decided to <u>write</u> a letter of complaint to the local <u>councillor</u>.
(iv) The <u>moral</u> of the story seemed to be that in the end people get what they deserve.
(v) As a child Kevin had always been <u>allowed</u> to do anything he wanted.
(vi) 'I can't read a word of this,' complained the teacher. 'You <u>write</u> in a completely <u>illegible</u> way.'
(vii) After years of having to work increasingly long hours the <u>morale</u> of the workforce was very low.
(viii) Anyone who wants to be a professional musician has to <u>practise</u> for several hours every day.
(ix) Accidents can occur when a pedestrian suddenly steps out from behind a <u>stationary</u> vehicle.
(x) It was a good idea in theory, but it was difficult to put into <u>practice</u>.

Page 85

THERE, THEIR and THEY'RE
(i) <u>There's</u> no point in asking if you can borrow <u>their</u> mobile phone. They'll never let you have it.
(ii) If <u>their</u> train's running to time, <u>they're</u> due to arrive about 7 pm.
(iii) <u>There's</u> only one route into the village: a long winding path up the hillside.
(iv) 'O Christmas Tree, O Christmas Tree, your branches green delight us. <u>They're</u> green when summer days are bright; <u>They're</u> green when winter snow is white.'

Page 86

Words confused because of the use of apostrophes
(i) <u>It's</u> nearly time for Santa to come.
(ii) <u>Whose</u> is the present with the red bow on it?
(iii) The weather forecast says <u>it's</u> going to be a white Christmas.
(iv) <u>Who's</u> going to help put up the Christmas decorations?
(v) Are you going to hang up <u>your</u> stocking on Christmas Eve?
(vi) Every year the store puts up a giant Christmas tree in <u>its</u> toy department.